CHRISTUS
LUX MUNDI

To Our Mothers

WILLIAM AND PATRICIA WILLIMON

Turning the World Upside Down

The Story of Sarah and Angelina Grimke

With Drawings by G. HOYT SIMMONS

columbia / sandlapper press
1972

FIRST EDITION

Published by Sandlapper Press, Inc.,
P.O. Box 1668, Columbia, S.C. 29202
Manufactured in the United States of America

International Standard Book Number: 0-87844-011-9
Library of Congress Catalog Card Number: 72-86901

Contents

Illustrations

1

Black Hands

It will be nice to be in Charleston again," said Sarah aloud as the Grimke' carriage rumbled along the rough country road.

Her brother Thomas had been leaning out the carriage window, gazing blankly into the dark swamp through which they were riding. Turning to his younger sister, Thomas replied, "You're glad to be moving back to the city because you're a girl. Girls are happier in Charleston than boys are. You like the parties and music lessons and Sunday school–and visits with our dull cousins. All that bores me. I like country life better."

"You don't like it because you're the worst dancer in your class," Sarah giggled.

"That's not true," retorted Thomas in an offended tone. "On the plantation there are more exciting things than dancing lessons. Hunting, fishing, crabbing, swimming in the creek, horse racing–I could go on forever."

"There's no use arguing with you," said Sarah, perhaps remembering the fact that Thomas was six years older than she and, since he was a boy, could out-shout her in any argument. "We should have let you stay in Beaufort for the summer where you could catch swamp fever. That would have served you right."

Sarah had a reputation for hardheadedness, and

Thomas also knew there was no use arguing. He pulled out a book from behind the carriage seat and began to read, and Sarah resumed her favorite pastime—simply sitting back and staring up at the sky to pass the time away.

Somehow Sarah always lost these arguments over whether it was better to be a boy or a girl. In the back of her mind she couldn't help wondering if it might not have been better if she had been born a boy. She still grew angry every time she thought about last Christmas.

Her mind wandered back to Christmas morning. She remembered waking up to the smell of Christmas puddings and cakes, drifting out from the kitchen. Her younger brothers and sisters were already up, dancing around the tree. But the most exciting moment of all was when the family gathered to open their presents.

Excitedly, Sarah had torn the bright paper and ribbon from her presents: a pair of satin slippers which her father had brought from Philadelphia, a beautiful china doll from England, a little ivory fan which she could use at parties next spring. But then, to Sarah's bewilderment, her eyes were not on her own presents. Rather they had wandered over to where her brother Thomas was opening his gifts.

There, in the confusion of wrappings and new treasures, Sarah saw the gift she wished had been hers—a small, leather-bound Latin book. She watched as Thomas proudly displayed his gift, a book which held the secrets of an ancient language, spoken centuries ago. Sarah knew that when Thomas had mastered Latin he would be able to enter college and become a learned man. That little book would be the key to her brother's future.

Why, she asked herself, should she envy her brother's gift? After all, as her mother had lectured her on many occasions, "All a polite Southern lady needs to know is sewing, needlework, a little music, and a little drawing and dancing. Anything more," Mrs. Grimke' declared, "would be a strain upon the gentle feminine mind."

Her sisters, Mary and Eliza, seemed satisfied with their mother's opinions. They were content to become "polite ladies." But this was not enough for Sarah. As Christmas wore on, she could not get Thomas' book out of her mind. Try as she would, she could not banish it with ivory fans and china dolls.

Finally she had made up her mind. Timidly, but with determination, Sarah had approached her father and asked him for permission to join Thomas in his Latin lessons.

Judge Grimké's face showed his astonishment. "Preposterous! Who ever heard of a polite young lady studying Latin?"

"But father," pleaded Sarah, "I know that I can do it. I have been able to master my other subjects as well as Thomas."

Her father had refused to listen. The whole family was convinced that further education would be useless for a girl, and even Thomas had failed to support her. Sadly, Sarah yielded.

As she left the room, Judge Grimke' smiled and thought to himself, "Too bad Sarah is not a boy. She would have made an excellent lawyer. She knows how to argue."

"Well," Sarah told herself, coming back to the present, "there are other things for me to learn." In an hour or so the carriage would be entering Charleston, and she would be returning to her family's town house on stately Church Street. Here they would be near the cool sea breeze and out of the disease-ridden swamps of the back country.

In Charleston there would be balmy evenings spent watching the fine ladies and gentlemen as they danced at one of the city's nightly parties. "Perhaps," thought Sarah, "I may be asked out by some gentleman for an afternoon stroll through the city. After all, I am eleven years old."

Sarah knew she was not a particularly pretty girl, but she enjoyed other people and they seemed to enjoy her cheerful, outgoing manner. Her mother had always told her that one's family was the most important factor in finding a suitable beau. If that were really the case, Sarah thought, she should have no trouble in attracting a fine gentleman. Her father had fought under General Washington in the Revolution, and he was not only a wealthy planter, but had also served his state as a Supreme Court Justice. He had even been mayor of Charleston. Her mother also came from a well-respected Carolina family, with two colonial governors among her ancestors. It was all a bit boring to think about, and as the carriage rolled on, Sarah slowly dropped off to sleep.

She was awakened by the sound of the wheels bumping over Charleston's cobblestone streets. She and Thomas leaned forward, each trying to be the first to see the spire of St. Philip's. Tall-masted ships stood along the docks, bringing goods from all over the world to exchange for bales of fine Carolina cotton and sacks of Carolina rice. Fish vendors sold their catches along the streets. As the carriage rumbled on, the gentle fragrance of camellias drifted from behind the walled gardens of wealthy homes. Prosperous planters strolled down the street, tipping their hats toward the Grimkés as they approached. Somehow Sarah felt that this was going to be an especially good summer, and she was glad to be back with her friends, back to the excitement of the city.

The train of carriages came to a stop in front of the Grimkés' town house, and Thomas jumped out. A dozen black hands reached out to help the Grimké girls from their seats; others unloaded trunks and bundles. A large Negro woman stood at the door, arms outstretched toward Sarah. "Mauma!" Sarah shouted as she bounded toward the old woman. "Mauma" was the Grimkés' nurse; she had helped raise all the children.

There was only one flaw to those pretty scenes of Sarah Grimké's life in Beaufort and Charleston. The hands which reached for her family's luggage, the hands which rocked the little Grimké children to sleep at night, which prepared their food and toiled in their father's fields, were black hands. And these black hands—slaves' hands—were an ever present reminder to Sarah Grimké that life was not as it should be.

The cause of Sarah Grimké's sadness was much older than she. The system of slavery had been over a hundred years old when she was born, and while slavery was practiced in nearly every state in the Union, few states relied as heavily upon slave labor as did South Carolina. The wealth of the South came from black labor. Behind the stately mansions and towering church spires of Charleston lay a tragic institution of human servitude. Along the coast black people outnumbered whites by nearly five to one.

Sarah's father owned hundreds of slaves. Since the invention of Eli Whitney's cotton gin, cotton production was growing more profitable, and slaves were auctioned daily on the streets of Charleston. The city's newspapers were filled with advertisements for new shipments of Negroes from Africa, as well as descriptions of runaway slaves who were being hunted. The demand for and the price of slaves were increasing. As Judge Grimke' expanded his cotton lands and augmented his slave holdings, his wealth grew accordingly.

In keeping with their position in society, the Grimke' family had a large staff of household servants—parlor maids, cleaning women, cooks, butlers, coachmen, stable boys, grooms for the horses—all slaves. Since Mrs. Grimke' was often busy overseeing her household or visiting friends and relatives, the work of raising the small children was usually left to Mauma. Sarah loved Mauma dearly. She felt even closer to her than she did to her own mother, and it had come as a great shock to her when she first realized that this kind old woman was a slave and a piece of property, like all other black people in her world.

Yet, as Sarah had observed during her family's stay on their plantation in Beaufort, the work of the household slaves was easy compared to that of the field hands, who did the back-breaking work of cotton cultivation. The slaves on the plantation had to work from early morning to late evening under the hot sun. Women and men worked alongside one another, and slave children were usually taken to the fields as soon as they could walk. Slaves who worked the rice fields had the worst job. They had to bend over in knee-deep, murky water all day, tending the young rice plants. The

rice paddies were infested with insects and disease, and few rice workers lived very long under these circumstances.

The fate of the cotton workers was somewhat better, but it was still hot, tedious work with few rewards. Sarah had heard white planters argue that only black men were fit for such work, but the high death rate of field hands made it obvious, to her at least, that few men, black or white, could withstand such conditions.

For the most part, Sarah had little contact with the slaves in the field. Yet she heard them moving out in the early morning, just as she was waking up. And in the evening, when she was already in bed, she could hear their solemn work songs and spirituals as they returned from their long days in her father's fields.

Like her brothers and sisters, like her friends, Sarah Grimké had been born into an old, established slave society. Much of the prosperity of her city and state was dependent upon the practice. Why did she, unlike many, come to question the morality of slavery?

One summer evening Sarah sat swinging with a young friend. "What one thing," her friend asked, "would you change if you ruled the world?"

Sarah answered without a moment's hesitation. "I would decree that there be no more slavery."

"No more slavery?" her companion asked, surprised. "Why? It isn't so bad being a slave. Ours are well treated. Father says they are all very happy and very lazy. They have someone to look after them for the rest of their lives and haven't a care in the world."

"We know only part of slavery. We have seen only the best of it," Sarah asserted. Her mind rushed back to a day many years ago, when she was only four. Playing in the garden, she had heard screams coming from behind the garden wall.

"In my childish curiosity," Sarah told her friend, "I peeped through the fence. There I saw my father's overseer brutally whipping a slave girl. I will never forget the awful look on her face as long as I live. Mauma found me an hour later down at the Charleston wharf, begging a sea captain to take me someplace where there was no slavery."

"But you can't judge all slavery by one bad incident," argued her friend. "Most slaves are treated well. Besides, they have never known any better."

"That's easy for you to say," replied Sarah, "but even at its best slavery is a degrading system. Few of us can look upon them as human beings. They are just property to be bought and sold, as far as our parents are concerned."

Sarah's mind again wandered back to her early childhood.

"A few years ago my father gave me a little black girl to wait on me. He told her to obey all of my orders and attend to my needs."

"I have a maid, too," interrupted her friend. "isn't it fun to have someone comb your hair each morning and play with you whenever you want?"

"I don't think it's such fun," replied Sarah. "Despite what my father said, I never considered my maid as anything but a good friend. I didn't want to be her mistress. But then the little girl died. I cried all night, but my parents didn't seem to understand."

" 'She was only a little servant girl,' my father said.

'I'll get you another one tomorrow. You can have your pick of any of the slave girls.'

"The very idea that my friend was nothing more than a piece of property, something to be cast aside like a broken toy, was too much for me to stand. To this day I have refused to choose another girl to serve me. I want no part of this cruel system."

Sarah's friend didn't know what to think of her strange ideas. "You are making too much of all of this," she said. "Certainly there are some bad things about slavery, but you and I did not begin the practice, and I doubt that we will be able to end it. Besides, without slavery we wouldn't have any of the nice things we have now. The best thing for you to do is grow up and learn to either accept slavery or keep silent about your dislike of it."

"I will not accept slavery and I will not keep silent," retorted Sarah. And that was that.

2

Precious Nina

When Sarah was twelve, Thomas left home to study at Yale College. As her brother prepared to depart for his exciting adventure, Sarah sadly prepared herself for the family's yearly removal to Beaufort. No matter how much she hungered for knowledge, it was Thomas who was going to have an education, while she would be forced to remain at home, filling her day with the trivial duties of a "polite lady."

"Why has God given brains to both boys and girls, if only boys are to be allowed to use them?" she asked herself.

But for now Sarah resigned herself to the fact that her dreams were not to be realized, and she decided to content herself with what she could do in the little world which had been allotted to her.

Each Sunday the Grimkés joined other prominent Charleston residents for service at St. Philip's Episcopal Church. Religion was a serious matter in the Grimké household. Sarah and her brothers and sisters were required to be at church every Sunday, unless they were ill. The Grimkés sat in their family pew and listened as the minister spoke of Hell's damnation for those who sinned and Heaven's reward for those who did good deeds and loved their God and their fellowmen. The household slaves sat crowded into the slaves' balcony, listening to the same sermon.

Every Sunday afternoon the Grimke girls taught Bible classes in the Sabbath School for slave children. Sarah enjoyed her teaching, but once again she was dissatisfied with the way things were done. She saw the eagerness of the slave children to learn.

"Why can't I teach them to read the Bible for themselves, rather than simply reading it to them one day a week?" Sarah asked.

Her parents were quick to answer. "Slaves have no use for reading, my dear," her father explained. "Reading only makes them restless and rebellious. Their barbaric minds are not fit for such pursuits. Reading would strain their minds and eventually make them unfit for the labors which they must perform. Besides," he added, "teaching slaves to read is strictly against the law."

Sarah could hardly believe what she heard. How could it be against the law? Nevertheless, it was true. Judge Grimke went into his library and took down the law book containing the 1740 act; clearly it stated that slaves were not to be taught to read or write.

"Apparently," thought Sarah to herself, "It is all right for slaves to hear the minister repeat the Apostle Paul's words, 'Slaves, obey your masters,' but our laws make it impossible for them to ever hear Jesus' teaching that all men are brothers and equal before God."

Although on the surface Sarah did submit to her father's wishes, she did not accept the rule completely.

Maria, a little slave girl in the Grimke' household, continued to beg Sarah to teach her to read. "Please teach me, Miss Sarah, so that I too can know what those strange pages mean."

Late at night, when Sarah was supposed to be asleep with Maria beside her, the two young rebels would stuff the keyhole with cotton and lie flat on their stomachs before the smoldering fire, a spelling book before them. Maria was a quick learner, and Sarah felt better now that she was helping someone else.

But the little rebellion soon ended. Late one night Mrs. Grimke' heard strange voices coming from Sarah's room:

"Israel, I-S-R-A-E-L. Children, C-H-I-L-D-R-E-N."

Mrs. Grimke' threw open the door and found the two of them before the fire with the book. Maria barely escaped a whipping. Sarah was summoned before her father and given a stern lecture.

"South Carolina stands under constant threat of slave rebellion," Judge Grimke' began, "and we masters must carefully guard what our slaves are taught. It is my responsibility to see that my own slaves are well supervised and guarded. Someday it will be your responsibility."

"But Father," Sarah pleaded, "it is a responsibility which I do not want."

"That may be so, my dear, but you have been born into this house in this state. When you are older, you will better understand the problems which we face. Until then I must demand that you give me your complete obedience as far as the slaves are concerned."

For a time it seemed as if Sarah had resigned herself to the pattern which her elders had chosen for her. She was nearly thirteen now, and her parents hoped that her rebelliousness had been broken.

But on the night of February 20, 1805, an event occurred which was to change Sarah's life. Mrs. Grimké gave birth to her last child, a daughter. Sarah begged to be given some responsibility for the baby. Her mother was ill and tired, and although it was not the custom, her parents decided to make Sarah the godmother of the new baby, hoping that the responsibility would give Sarah a much-needed sense of usefulness.

A few weeks later the Grimkés brought their child to St. Philip's for the christening ceremony.

"I baptize thee, Angelina Emily Grimké," repeated the minister. "And to you, Sarah, I make you her godmother. Do you vow to train this child in the ways of the Christian faith?"

"With God's help, I will," replied Sarah.

That night, alone in her room, Sarah earnestly prayed, "Oh God, make me worthy of this task. Make me careful in my conduct, so that my life may be a blessing to this little one."

The new baby became the purpose and hope of Sarah Grimké's life.

As Sarah grew to adulthood, the baby in her care—"Precious Nina," as Sarah called her – gave her constant pleasure. To Sarah's delight the baby even called her "Mother."

"That child will grow up to be more like Sarah than any of us," her father would say, and Angelina's life was to prove the truth of that prediction. When not tending Angelina, Sarah read books on various subjects and wrote frequent letters to Thomas. She was happier now than she could ever remember.

Thomas' three years at Yale passed quickly and he returned to Charleston. Sarah listened excitedly as her brother told of all the new ideas circulating around the Northern campus—dangerous European philosophies, modern theories of education, scientific discoveries.

Thomas had been influenced by the religious revival which had swept Yale, and one night he revealed to Sarah his decision to become a minister.

"But what will you tell father?" Sarah asked. "You know he has always wanted you to become a lawyer."

"That may be a problem," admitted Thomas. "But I will be firm in my desire to follow the career for which I am called."

Thomas's boldness inspired Sarah to tell her brother her secret desire. "Thomas," she said, "what would you say if I told you I wanted to be a lawyer? What would you say if I told you I have been secretly studying Father's law books for some time now? I think that I could do it, especially if you would help me in my studies."

But Thomas gave Sarah little support. "Surely you know you would face overwhelming odds," he told her. "I don't know of a school in the country which would admit a woman to advanced study. Besides," he added half in jest, "who would allow a woman to argue a case in court?"

As it turned out, Thomas himself proved unable to stand up to his domineering father. Only a few months after he had returned from Yale, he was preparing himself for his future career—not as a minister, but as the lawyer his father wanted him to be.

Seeing her older brother bow to the will of their father, Sarah gave up all hope of studying law. If

Thomas had failed to choose his future, what chance had she of choosing hers? Left with nothing but a bitter disappointment, Sarah never again mentioned her secret dream. Years later she wrote, "With me learning was always a passion, . . . but my aspirations were crushed."

While Thomas entered upon a career in law, Sarah entered society. At the age of sixteen she found herself caught up in the gay whirl of Charleston social life. In the morning she would go for a stroll in the garden, or teach little Nina a few elementary reading lessons. In the afternoon there were teas, visits with friends, or walks along the Battery. Sometimes she would join other young socialites for a picnic on Sullivan's Island. In the evening there were parties, an occasional ball, or simply long discussions with friends after dinner. In her diary she recorded her total absorption in Charleston life.

And yet Sarah was never a real part of such gaiety. Her sensibilities did not fit the role of the Charleston belle. One evening after a ball she wrote in her diary: "I returned home almost ill. I am sick of the frivolous people I have been with, mortified at my own folly, and weary of the ball-room and its guilded toys. Night after night as I have been glittering in this gay scene my soul has been disturbed by the biblical question, 'What are you doing with the talents committed to thy charge?' "

It was also during these years that her brother was married. From then on Sarah and Thomas saw very little of one another. He had his own life now; soon he would have his own family. Her other brothers, John and Fred, were starting their careers, John as a doctor and Fred as a lawyer. But what of her life? Still she thought of a career, while her parents thought of marriage.

Time and again Mrs. Grimké had said, "Sarah, I don't

want any spinster daughters. You know how pleased your father and I would be if you found yourself a suitable sweetheart from one of Charleston's proper families." But the prospect of marriage and life as the mistress of a typical Charleston household held little appeal for Sarah. Her mind traveled too far, her questions were too deep, her sensibilities were too strong to accept such a future.

There were other forces at work which troubled Sarah's mind. The spectre of slavery was always before her. One spring afternoon, while the family was on the plantation in Beaufort, Sarah went for a ride along a country road. As the coach rumbled along the bumpy road, Sarah heard the horrified cry of her coachman, "Look there, Miss Sarah, don't you see–"

Sarah looked up at a pole which had been planted beside the road. There was a severed human head at the top of the pole, the head of an unfortunate slave who had run away from a neighboring plantation and whose fate had been put on display as a warning to other slaves. Sarah turned away in horror and ordered the coachman on.

It seemed as if each day Sarah discovered even more cruel aspects of the slave system. One afternoon, at tea with a group of her friends, she was shocked to hear a girl from one of the "finest families of Charleston," describing an invention which she had devised.

"I have solved the problem of punishing troublesome slaves," the girl boasted.

Sarah sat in silence, preparing for the worst.

"I suggested to my father that he fasten a strap around the slave's neck, tying the end of the strap around one of the slave's raised ankles, and then have the slave stand upright on his other foot for an hour."

"But the least bit of weight on the foot which is tied to the strap would cause the slave to choke," cried Sarah.

"That is the purpose of the invention," replied her cruel friend.

Before Sarah could answer, another friend had begun, "My mother says that the best thing to do to a slave who steals is to have the slave's ears slit. That way the other slaves will be reminded of what they will have to suffer if they should steal."

"But you treat these Negroes as if they were not human beings," charged Sarah in a horrified voice.

"Well are they?" one of the girls asked. "They rarely act like human beings."

"Negroes are basically lazy, deceitful, and slovenly," another chimed in. "The person to be pitied is the white master who has to endure such trifling servants."

Such open cruelty was one thing, but blind hypocrisy in the treatment of slaves seemed almost worse to Sarah. One day she visited in the home of a family friend who was known all over the city for her Christian piety and charitable work.

Upon entering the home, Sarah happened to glance into a side room. There, sitting on a pile of filthy rags, was a wretched slave girl. Not only did the girl bear the marks of repeated whippings, but she also wore a heavy iron collar with three long prongs projecting from it. The collar made it virtually impossible for the girl to move about or rest her head.

"What has happened to this girl?" asked Sarah, openly shocked.

"That girl has been nothing but a bother to us,"

replied her hostess. "After she repeatedly ran away and we repeatedly whipped her, my husband devised this contraption for her to wear. The next time she tries to run away I am going to have her front teeth pulled out so she will be easier to identify. Slaves are truly a burden to white people."

Sarah could scarcely speak. How could this supposedly Christian woman feel no compassion for this poor girl? She left the house, determined never to visit there again.

Not all slaveholders practiced such brutality on their slaves, and some masters prided themselves on their kind treatment of slaves. But as Sarah later remarked, even in its best aspects slavery was still a degrading, inhuman system. Still, if she herself could not hide from the horrors of slavery, at least, thought Sarah, she might be able to keep little Angelina from seeing them. She did not succeed.

One day Angelina was brought home from school, where she had fainted for no apparent reason. No one had been able to find out what had happened. Sarah took Angelina up to her room, and there, when the two were alone, her little sister told her.

"It was awful," sobbed Angelina. "During school a little slave boy who belongs to one of the children in my class had been asked by our teacher to raise the window. The little boy is about my age. I looked up from my book and noticed that he could barely walk across to the window. I wondered what was wrong with him. When he turned his back to the class, I saw what the trouble was."

Angelina could barely go on. "The poor little boy had long scars across his back and the backs of his legs.

Some of the wounds were still bleeding. It was the worst sight I have ever seen. Oh Sarah, why do people do these things to other people?"

Sarah could not answer. She had no words of comfort for her little sister, because she had the same terrible feelings in her own heart. Angelina's pretty little world had collapsed in much the same way that hers had, and she had no answers herself.

"I too have seen the cruelties of slavery, Angelina. I too have felt what you now feel, but we were born into a world that we did not create. There is little that you or I can do about it. We must simply make the best of our world as we have found it."

Sarah wept with her sister. Angelina seemed consoled, but she was old enough and knew her sister well enough to know that Sarah did not really believe what she was telling her.

3

First Farewell

Sarah's mother continued to fret over her daughter's inability to attract some eligible young gentleman, although by now Mrs. Grimké had almost resigned herself to the fact that Sarah might be headed for a life of spinsterhood. Sarah was popular; she had a good family and an excellent mind; but nature had not endowed her with pleasant looks or a beautiful face. Few young men came to call at the Grimké household for plain Sarah.

Sarah was not at all disturbed by her marital situation. She was now twenty-four, and by now she had decided that she would never be chosen for courtship. She occupied herself by assisting Nina with her lessons, helping her mother manage the household, and taking part in church and charitable activities.

Sarah took her religion seriously. She was "converted" by an eloquent Presbyterian minister on several occasions, and these emotional stirrings of faith led her to more strenuous attempts to improve her religious life. She spent many hours each day in prayer and Bible reading, examining every aspect of her life to make sure that her morals were beyond reproach. She gave up novels, parties, dancing and picnics, thereby virtually ending her participation in Charleston social life. Still, she was plagued by a nagging sense of personal guilt and unworthiness.

In 1818, Judge Grimke' fell seriously ill, and Sarah devoted herself to constant care of her ailing father. When Charleston doctors advised him to consult an eminent physician in Philadelphia, it was decided that Sarah should accompany him on the long journey. In the spring of 1819 they sailed for Philadelphia.

But neither Sarah nor her father realized just how ill he was. The Philadelphia doctor had advised Judge Grimke' to spend a few weeks recuperating at the New Jersey seashore, but by the time they reached their destination Judge Grimke' was deathly ill. Sarah attended her father day and night. He was never well enough even to leave his bed and look out the window at the sea.

"You must get some rest, my child," he urged Sarah in a strained voice.

"Father, I will not leave your side. I am praying for your recovery," she told him.

"Do not indulge vain hopes, Sarah. I no longer expect to recover, nor do I desire it."

Sarah fought back the tears as she realized that her father was dying. In a few days, Judge John Faucheraud Grimke', planter, lawyer, statesman and father, was dead. Despite her grief, Sarah remained strong throughout the ordeal. She was no stranger to death, having nursed sick relatives and servants before, and having laid many to their final rest. Life was short in those days.

Alone among strangers in a strange place, Sarah laid her father to rest in a little New Jersey cemetery, far from his beloved Carolina. Then she started her lonely journey home. A familiar part of her world had slipped away. Sarah's father had always been a tower of strength to her; now he was gone.

Aboard ship on her homeward journey, Sarah was befriended by a group of Quakers, members of an old religious group who had settled mostly around Philadelphia. One of the Quakers, Israel Morris, a successful businessman from Philadelphia, comforted Sarah and explained to her the Quaker doctrines.

"From what you have told me about yourself," Morris said, "I think that you might find many of our beliefs to be your beliefs too."

"Mr. Morris, I do not know what my beliefs are now," confided Sarah, gazing out across the ocean. "There is nothing that I can be sure of. Now, with my father gone, I seem to have nothing even to live for."

"My dear woman, there is much to live for. It is our belief that God inspires us and guides us in the right direction for our lives. We have to be silent and let him speak."

Sarah became more interested in the quiet confidence of this man. "What has God spoken to you? What purpose do you see for your life, Mr. Morris?"

Israel Morris answered. "He has shown me that there is much to do in the world. As long as there is war, we can help to bring peace. As long as there is slavery, we can work for freedom."

"And what do you Quakers believe about slavery?" she questioned, hoping to hear an answer that might help her decide.

"I must be frank," replied Morris. "We Quakers have always believed that slavery is a sin against God and a crime to our fellowmen.'"

His words made a strong impression on Sarah. She

JOHN
FAUCHERAUD
GRIMKÉ
1752-1819

could hardly hold back her joy at having finally heard someone speak boldly against the evil of slavery. When she disembarked at Charleston, she agreed to write Israel Morris, and he agreed to send her more information about the Quakers.

Sarah returned to her home on Church Street to find the entire household in deep mourning. Thy doorway where Judge Grimke' used to stand and wave to passersby on the street was now draped in black. The family had lost its father, and the slaves had lost their master.

Many of his slaves had grown to love Judge Grimké, and many now feared that since the master's death there might be a sale of slaves, splitting families as they were sold to different buyers; some might even be bought by cruel masters. In his will Judge Grimke' had left his wife nearly all of his possessions and any five Negroes of her choice. The rest were to be distributed among the Grimke' children who were married, or sold at auction.

After the estate was settled, Sarah had time to write Israel Morris. She had read the writings of John Woolman, a Quaker who had denounced slavery as "the worst of all human sins." Since her conversations with Morris, she realized that the question of slavery was constantly on her mind. Now, more than ever, she was tortured by the thought that she and her loved ones were living on the forced toil of these pitiful human beings.

Angelina, now a popular girl of fourteen, often discussed the slavery issue with Sarah. Though neither had yet firmly decided upon the question, it was clear that both of them were deeply troubled by it.

One day when they were alone with Thomas, they

asked him his opinions on slavery. After all, they thought, Thomas should know the right way to deal with the problem.

"I will freely admit the evils of the system," he said, "and I agree with you that slavery is a curse upon our state."

"The Quakers have proposed that slaves should be set free," ventured Sarah.

"That's ridiculous," said Thomas, laughing. "The impracticality of those holy Quakers! The main consideration is, what is the most realistic and practical way to solve the problem? Merely to stop the buying, selling, and holding of slaves would hardly be a practical solution. What would be done with the free slaves?"

"Couldn't they simply live here with us, farming and working as they do now?" suggested Angelina.

"My dear Angelina, you know so little of these things," chided Thomas. Angelina was a bit hurt by this rebuff. "There is no way that white men will ever live with black men in peace. The only way white men will ever accept the black man is as a slave, so the only practical way to free the slaves is to devise some scheme of removing them from our land. No Southerners would tolerate large numbers of free Negroes in their midst."

"But how could we ever hope to remove all the thousands of black people among us?" asked Sarah, astonished at the very magnitude of the task.

"Luckily, some of us are working on such a plan," explained Thomas. "The American Colonization Society has been founded for the purpose of removing free Negroes to a colony in Africa. We hope to encourage masters to free their slaves, on the condition that the freed slaves will be transported out of this country.

Thus emancipation of the slaves would be accomplished in a way that white men could accept."

"But how," asked Angelina, feeling bold once again, "will the planters be persuaded to give up their slaves?"

"There are a few problems yet to be ironed out," admitted Thomas, realizing that his sister had hit upon the main weakness of the scheme.

Thomas failed to convert his sisters to his theories. "I think the Colonization Society is more interested in the wishes of whites than in the good of blacks," was Sarah's final verdict.

As Israel Morris continued to correspond with Sarah, she became more attracted to the Quaker faith. She even mustered enough courage to attend Quaker meetings in Charleston. Her family strongly disapproved, and Thomas teased her, but by this time Sarah had gone too far to turn back. She was already too accustomed to acting and thinking alone to be deterred from doing what she believed God wanted her to do.

Eventually the moment came when Sarah approached Mrs. Grimke' with a painful decision. "Mother, I have heard inner voices. They have told me to go to Philadelphia, in order to study and become a Quaker. Israel and Catherine Morris have asked me to live with them."

Mrs. Grimke' was hardly surprised. "I expected that you'd be hearing those 'inner voices' before too long," she said. "Although I don't approve of your strange religious ideas, I know that there is no stopping you. But I must tell you," she added, "that your unorthodox opinions have become an increasing source of embarrassment for your family."

"I am sorry if I cause you pain," replied Sarah. "You

know I love you all. I appreciate your willingness to let me go."

Sarah's mother told the polite ladies of Charleston that her daughter was taking a "short trip to the North for reasons of health." But in her heart Mrs. Grimke' knew that Sarah's separation was permanent. It was a step for which Sarah had been unconsciously preparing for a long time. She had come to realize that she did not fit into the Southern way of life. Giving up all hope of being able to change the things she disliked about her home, she felt that she had only one alternative left: to cut herself free and start out anew.

Although she would return to Charleston for several short visits, in her heart Sarah Grimke' left Charleston forever in May 1821.

4

Dark Dreams

Angelina eagerly awaited the arrival of letters from her older sister in Philadelphia. Sarah wrote that she was happily settled and had made a number of good friends among the Quakers. Before long Sarah had adopted the simple dress of the Quakers. Angelina loved colorful capes and bright bonnets, and she was horrified at the thought of her sister dressed in the sombre black dresses of Quaker women. Yet Sarah assured Angelina that the dress of the Quakers suited her well, and that she was happy to be admitted into their religious community.

By this time Angelina was a popular girl of eighteen. She had been indulged and pampered by her family from birth, and from an early age she had been known as a strong-willed, determined young lady. Unlike Sarah, who kept her secret ambitions and doubts to herself, Angelina was entirely self-confident in everything she undertook. Frequently she shocked her elders by her indifference to their standards. Still, Mrs. Grimké suspected that some of Angelina's strong-mindedness must have come from Sarah's influence. She was right.

At the age of thirteen, when the time came for Angelina's confirmation into the membership of St. Philip's, she dumbfounded the rector by declaring her disagreement with parts of the Anglican Creed in her prayer book.

"Because I disagree with the pledge, I cannot take the vows of membership," she told the astonished minister. "If I should go through with it, I would be acting a lie. I cannot do it."

"But what will your parents say? What will the church say? Indeed, what will the whole city say?" he asked. Angelina remained firm in her refusal.

By the time she was twenty-one, Angelina had come under the influence of a local Presbyterian minister, one Mr. McDowell, and had been converted to Presbyterianism. Mrs. Grimke' asked the minister of St. Philip's to make one last effort to bring Angelina back into the Episcopal fold, but her strong-minded daughter rejected his efforts.

"The main thing that attracts me to the Presbyterian church," she wrote Sarah, "is its liberal attitude. It does not set itself above other churches. It does not refuse to let ministers from other denominations use its pulpits. Presbyterians are more interested in godliness than displays of finery."

Angelina also wrote Sarah that she had organized a monthly prayer meeting for women from a number of different churches. Angelina's interfaith gathering of women shocked many people. It was not the last thing Angelina would give them to be shocked about.

Mr. McDowell was a native of New Jersey who had come South for reasons of health. He had strong reservations about slavery and praised Angelina's daily prayer meetings with the Grimke' family slaves. But Angelina pressed her minister further.

"If slavery is an evil, why do you permit members of

our congregation to hold slaves?" she asked him. "Can it be right for white Christians to hold black Christians in bondage?"

"I agree that slavery is morally wrong, Angelina. But you must be realistic," he told her. "Slavery is an entrenched institution. Pray and have patience, my dear."

"I will pray, but I cannot have patience with something which is wrong," was Angelina's reply. She urged Mr. McDowell to openly declare his views on slavery from his pulpit. He refused.

Although she was disappointed that Mr. McDowell chose the cautious path of silence, Angelina could understand, in a way, his hesitation. Of the few Southern ministers who had preached against slavery, nearly all had been silenced by their angry congregations. Most major religious denominations had decided that it was best to leave the controversial issue alone. Increased Northern criticism of slavery, the ever-present danger of slave revolts, rising cotton prices—all were leading Southerners to prohibit any discussion of the subject.

But compromise never suited Angelina's temperament. "If Mr. McDowell will not speak out," she thought, "I will undertake the job of persuasion alone."

At the next meeting of the officials of her church, all slaveholders, Angelina came before them and suggested that they should lead the church in speaking out against slavery.

"You are our Christian leaders," she boldly lectured them. "You must show the way for the rest of our people to follow."

The elders listened politely to her request, then

replied. "If you were older, you would understand how we feel." Not surprisingly, they rejected her request.

In her next letter to Sarah, Angelina wrote, "I have not yet given up. I have spoken to a number of individual church members on the subject—but I must admit with little success."

Angelina was slowly becoming disillusioned with her church, and she listened more receptively to Sarah's descriptions of Quakerism. After Sarah's brief visit to Charleston in 1827, Angelina found herself drifting even closer toward the Quakers. She began to wear more simple dress and spend more time alone in meditation. One Sunday, while her mother and sisters drove off to St. Philip's in their fine carriage, Angelina set out on foot for Charleston's Quaker meeting house.

Mr. McDowell soon called upon her in an attempt to win her back to Presbyterianism. She listened to his arguments and his quotes from scripture, then bluntly told him why she must leave his church.

"I cannot continue to worship with Christians who seem to have Christian feelings only toward other Christians of the same color."

Mr. McDowell pleaded no more. He knew that he could make no excuse for his congregation's attitudes toward slavery. He had lost Angelina to the Quakers. A summer vacation spent with Sarah in Philadelphia only strengthened her Quaker beliefs and anti-slavery sentiments.

Now all of Charleston was talking about Angelina. Rumors were abroad that another Grimké daughter had become "mentally unbalanced." Friends began to call on Mrs. Grimké to inquire about the state of Angelina's mental health.

"After all," they said, trying carefully not to offend Mrs. Grimké, "has not Angelina withdrawn from two churches? Has she not been scandalizing her family by broadcasting her outlandish opinions all over Charleston? And now this Quaker nonsense."

Undisturbed by the rumors, Angelina was as determined as ever to follow her conscience. But she was not yet ready to leave the South, still hoping she might be able to bring about some change.

She decided to reform her family first. Unfortunately, Angelina's reformation attempts usually took the form of arguments and fault-finding among her brothers and sisters. She nagged Henry so much about his personal habits that he decided to leave home rather than suffer her constant criticism. She enraged her sister Mary when she rebuked her for being cruel to her servants. Brother John refused to speak to Angelina at all.

The painful arguments with her mother increased. "Why is it that you and Sarah are always convinced that you are right and everyone else is wrong?" Mrs. Grimké would ask. "Your continual fault-finding with everyone is becoming unbearable. You have changed, Angelina. You have not always condemned slaveholding. Why is it that you now have such a sudden dislike for it?"

"Mother," cried Angelina, "you know I have always had misgivings about slavery. Only recently have I had the courage and the strength of conscience to speak my views."

"I think those Quakers have ruined you. Why is it that Quakers seem to see things as sins which most good people have no misgivings about at all?" Mrs. Grimké asked.

Angelina did not reply. She and her mother had grown too far apart. Mrs. Grimke' was too old and had lived with things as they were for too long to be able to change overnight. For her, Angelina's strong-mindedness had become a constant source of pain.

Everywhere she went, everything she saw reminded Angelina how different her attitudes were from those of most Charlestonians. A child in her Bible class was the daughter of the owner of one of Charleston's "workhouses." Angelina frequently visited the little girl, and occasionally she caught a glimpse of the horrors of the workhouse, where unruly or unmanageable slaves were sent for discipline by masters who were too dainty to whip them.

Here whippings were administered to male and female slaves alike in orderly fashion, but the most dreaded punishment was the treadmill, a drum covered with steps. The slave's hands were fastened to a handrail above the treadmill, then the drum was rotated at great speed. The slave had to tread as fast as he could so that he would not be struck on the knees or feet by the whirling drum. Fifteen minutes on this torture wheel and a slave would be crippled for days afterward. Angelina wrote to Sarah describing what she had seen:

These are not things that I have heard . . . my own eyes have looked upon them and wept over them . . . . No one can image my feelings walking down that street. It seemed as though I was walking on the very confines of hell. . . . I suffered so much that I could not get over it for days and wondered how any real Christian could live near such a place.

One morning, as Angelina was out shopping, she saw a black woman being dragged down the street by two white teenage boys. The woman was pleading with them. Angelina knew they were taking her to the workhouse for punishment. Walking quickly on, she tried to avoid the scene, but the black woman appealed to her, "Missis! Please help me." Angelina hurried past, ignoring the woman's plea. For many days her conscience was full of guilt for not stopping to help.

Slavery became an obsession with her. Night after night she dreamed of black hands bound in chains; she heard the cries of countless slaves whom she had known. It seemed as if all the scenes of cruelty and unkindness which she had seen since her infancy were now continually thrust before her mind. Turning to her diary, she wrote, "How long, oh Lord, wilt thou suffer the foot of the oppressor to stand on the neck of the slave!"

Angelina used every opportunity to bring up the issue of slavery. One day a group of her mother's friends were having tea at the Grimke' home. They were discussing their troublesome servants, their laziness, depravity and dishonesty. For a while Angelina listened, but she could not remain silent.

"Why do you think they act in this way?" she asked suddenly. "What makes them prone to dishonesty and theft?"

"Negroes were born that way," one of the ladies suggested. "They are naturally slovenly and degraded."

"I disagree," argued Angelina. "What chance have we given them to improve themselves? We prohibit them from reading. We do everything that we can to keep them in a degraded and servile condition. Why shouldn't they steal? We have stolen them from their homeland and now we steal not only their labor but also their humanity. Why shouldn't they refuse to work willingly? They get no reward for their efforts."

But this was too much for the Charleston lady to stand. "Young lady, I would appreciate it if you never speak again in such a tone. I find your manner most impudent," she said curtly.

"Angelina, I think that we have had enough," her mother added.

"The truth cuts deep into the heart," replied Angelina, leaving the room.

Each new day seemed to occasion a new argument over slavery. "Why must we continually order slaves up and down the stairs to open our windows, pick up our clothes, fetch us a cup of tea?" Angelina asked her mother. "Why must slaves be forced to sleep each night on the bare floor outside the mistress' bedroom and be awakened at any time to do the bidding of the mistress? Why do we sleep with mosquito nets over our beds and refuse to let the slaves have them over theirs?"

Brother Henry had a slave named John whom he often whipped. Angelina did not interfere, even when John showed her the deep scars across his back. One day the slave ran away. Henry was furious. "When I get that slave back I'll beat him so that he will never try this again," he declared.

"But Henry," Angelina protested, "that would be treating him worse than you would treat your own horse. Perhaps it is your cruelty which has induced him to run away."

Henry was furious. "As a matter of fact, I don't consider my horse a bit different from John. I probably wouldn't beat my horse as much as I do that slave." Angelina burst into tears.

Despite Henry's hard words, Angelina could tell she had made an impression on him. When John returned the next night, Henry dismissed him with only a short lecture and did not punish him at all. Angelina excitedly informed Sarah of what had happened. "My heart sings for joy," she wrote. "Dear Henry does have tender feelings. But a false education has nearly destroyed them."

But except for this small triumph Angelina knew she had labored against slavery for over a year without success. Her outspokenness and criticism had only caused her mother pain and had embarrassed the rest of her family. By now Sarah's letters had convinced Angelina that it was best if she, like her older sister, remove herself from her home.

When Angelina told her mother her decision to join Sarah in Philadelphia, once again Mrs. Grimke' admitted that she did not agree with their notions about slavery, but she knew that her daughters could never accept or be accepted in Charleston. "I only pray that you are right and that I am wrong, and that the Lord will make me able to see it," she said as Angelina prepared for her journey.

In November 1829, Angelina Emily Grimke' sailed from Charleston for her chosen exile in the North. As the boat sailed past Fort Sumter and the spires of Charleston sank into the distance, she felt a deep regret at leaving her home. Yet there seemed no other way. Her departure was seen by all who knew her as a public protest against slavery and against the society which refused to change.

5

The End of Everything

Stepping off the boat at Philadelphia, Angelina felt as if she were stepping into another world. Sarah and Catherine Morris were there to meet her. The ride from the dock to the Morris's home gave Angelina her first glimpse of everyday life in the "City of Brotherly Love."

They passed rows of quaint little brick houses, housewives shopping, craftsmen at work in their shops. Angelina was surprised to see white men working as carpenters, bricklayers and fish sellers. How strange that would seem in Charleston, where most white men considered it undignified to be employed in such menial work. She was pleased that here white men too lived by the sweat of their brows.

Sarah pointed out something else which made Philadelphia different from Charleston. Intermingled with the crowds along the street were Negro peddlers, vendors and fish sellers shouting their wares to passers-by. On the outside these black merchants looked much the same as the slaves in Charleston, and yet there was an important difference. These men were free. The money they made was theirs to keep. Although most of them were employed in lowly occupations, there was a dignity about them; their self-pride and manliness set

them apart from the degraded victims of Southern slavery.

Angelina soon became a happy member of the Morris household. At last her opinions were accepted rather than ridiculed. Her letters to her family were filled with enthusiasm for her new home and friends. Everything seemed better, brighter, bigger here.

The Quakers were kind and sympathetic toward the two exiles. Before long Angelina had applied for membership in the Quaker society. The men who examined her for membership were impressed by her devotion and piety, yet they questioned the correctness of her decision to leave her mother and come north. Angelina defended her actions. She told them of her efforts to convert her family and of her misery at having to live in the midst of slavery. Besides, her mother was in good health and had family and slaves to care for her when she needed it. The membership committee approved her application, yet Angelina was a bit ruffled by their hesitant attitude.

Among the Quakers there was much charitable activity but little diversion, for their religion solemnly prohibited such "vain amusements" as the theatre or dancing. Even a bright ribbon tied in the hair of a Quaker woman might bring forth severe criticism. Angelina and Sarah were models of the dutiful Quaker lady, filling their days with charitable activities. They visited the local jail and held prayer meetings with the inmates, took up collections for the poor and attended the sick. Sarah sought appointment as a Quaker minister, but the society refused her request. Many had doubts about a woman in such an elevated position. Sarah accepted their decision; after all, it was not the first time she had been turned down because she was not a man.

For the most part Sarah and Angelina were unaware of important events which were going on in the nation, events which were to affect their lives deeply in later years. It was through their brother Thomas that the sisters were first to be engaged in the political discussions of the day.

Strong feelings had been aroused between North and South over the Northern states' desire for a national tariff on certain imported manufactured goods. Northern merchants favored the tariff, since it would protect their manufactured products from foreign competition. The South, which had few factories, opposed the tariff since it would only force Southern farmers to pay more for what they bought. The Southern states claimed that a few Northern states had no right to force this tariff upon them.

Did a state have the right to refuse to obey a national law which had been passed by a majority of the other states? The struggle to answer that question was the beginning of open conflict between North and South. Most political leaders in South Carolina, men like Vice President of the United States John C. Calhoun and the Grimkes' fiery cousin, Robert Barnwell Rhett, claimed that South Carolina had the right to nullify the tariff law. Sometimes they even suggested that a state had the right to secede from the Union if it felt that its rights were being violated.

To a patriotic lover of the Union like Thomas Grimké, talk of nullification and secession was sheer treason. In a courageous letter to Calhoun, Thomas told the Vice President to put aside sectional feeling and stand behind the will of the Union. When Thomas's letter was made public, an angry mob gathered outside the Grimke' home. Thomas met the mob on the steps of his house, declaring, "I am ready to be mobbed for the cause of my beloved Union." The mob was impressed with Grimké's courage and dispersed.

From Philadelphia, Angelina and Sarah followed these events with excitement. Their brother's actions filled them with pride. Little did they know that this crisis was a grave warning of things to come.

Other significant events were occuring around the nation. On an October night in 1831, Nat Turner, a Negro who was thought by his followers to be a divinely inspired prophet, led a band of slaves in Southampton County, Virginia, in a brief armed uprising. During the course of one night the Negroes killed fifty-seven white persons, mostly women and children. The uprising was quickly and brutally surpressed. Hundreds of Negroes, many of whom had not even taken part in the revolt, were tortured or killed. A wave of panic swept over the South, where every town lived in fear lest other slaves would follow Turner's example.

Throughout the South opinion was solidifying in support of slavery and against those who criticized the slave system. Anti-slavery literature was banned, and after 1832, with few exceptions, slavery was no longer a debatable issue in the South.

Through all this ferment over slavery, Sarah and Angelina continued to labor at their local charities, showing little interest in the affairs of the nation. The anti-slavery movement had not yet come to their door.

Angelina was teaching in a girls' school in Philadelphia, but she soon became dissatisfied, feeling that she lacked enough education to teach effectively. In the summer of 1831 she visited Catherine Beecher's Female Seminary in Hartford, Connecticut. Miss Beecher, whose sister was later to become world-famous as the author of *Uncle Tom's Cabin,* had founded a fine school for girls and written a best-selling book on home economics. At her school, girls specialized in two or three subjects, learned the latest methods of teaching and used scientific approaches to domestic work. Angelina was impressed by the school and its founder. Catherine Beecher was an awe-inspiring example of female achievement, and living proof of the potential of women. Angelina decided to enroll in the seminary in the fall.

Upon her return to Philadelphia, she excitedly told her Quaker friends of her plans to return to Hartford. To her bewilderment, only Sarah thought it would be a good idea. The rest could not understand what she hoped to accomplish. Too many people still distrusted the idea of higher education for women.

Now Angelina, like Sarah before her, submitted to the will of their friends. "Perhaps they know what is best for me," she told herself. In her diary she justified her decision not to attend the school with a biblical quote: "Obedience is better than sacrifice."

Besides, Angelina now had other interests on her mind. A handsome young Quaker named Edward Bettle had begun courting her. He called on her every day, and soon the entire Quaker fellowship was buzzing over the romance. Angelina found herself thinking of a possible future with Edward. "I am not yet ready to resign myself to a life of lonely spinsterhood as Sarah has," she wrote in her diary. "Now that I have been checked in my attempts to start a career for myself, it would be best for me to find a mate and start a home." Friends knew it would be only a matter of weeks before Angelina and Edward announced their engagement.

Then tragedy struck. In the hot summer of 1832, a cholera epidemic swept over Philadelphia. Physicians told the city's residents to "remain tranquil in mind and body and prudent in living, wear flannel next to the skin, and eat no cucumbers or watermelons." This was little help. In the crowded city prison where Angelina and Sarah had held prayer meetings, 70 out of the 131 prisoners died. Quaker charitable societies distinguished themselves for their courageous work among victims of the epidemic, but by early fall 935 people had died of cholera in Philadelphia.

On the evening of September 24, when it seemed as if the cholera threat were lifting, Angelina attended a wedding at a Quaker meetinghouse. As she watched she imagined what she would look like, passing through the same ceremony.

The next morning Sarah knocked at Angelina's door. Messengers had come, Sarah told her, to report that Edward was gravely ill. Fearing the worst, the two sisters knelt and prayed for Edward's recovery. "Oh Lord," said Angelina, "I pray that thou wilt not take this blessing from me, this one hope of my life."

But their prayers were not answered. Edward died in a few days, and Angelina's dream of marriage ended. There was nothing left for her now except to join the little band of spinsters who lived together, exercising their love through religion and charity, burying their lost hopes in concern for others.

It was only natural in this period of sadness that Sarah and Angelina should turn to the one remaining source of strength in their lives, their brother Thomas. He had continued to involve himself in the great issues of his day, especially in his support of the Union. When other prominent Southern statesmen were preaching force and disunion, Thomas urged peace and restraint. They read of their brother's actions with pride, looking forward to his letters and the occasional books which he sent them.

Two years after Edward Bettle's death, Thomas visited Angelina and Sarah. The sisters, who had grown even firmer in their antislavery beliefs, criticized their brother's colonization views and urged him to examine their idea of immediate emancipation.

"I have been planning to study the subject for some time," Thomas admitted. "I just never seem to get around to it, with all my other interests."

"What more pressing issue could there be at this time?" asked Angelina. "Is this not the very question which threatens to split the Union? Is this not the question for which men of the South are now talking secession and violence and treason?"

"I must agree to the importance of the issue," said Thomas. "Perhaps you would be good enough to furnish me with some books on immediate emancipation. I will be traveling west soon, lecturing on new theories in education. I should have time to do some reading along the way."

Thomas left Philadelphia with a stack of books and the hopes of his sisters that his views would be changed. From Philadelphia he traveled throughout Ohio, lecturing to large crowds. During the tour, Thomas fell sick and had to be put to bed at a small stage stop. He died on November 2 of Asiatic cholera—alone, in a small room in the Ohio backcountry. His final judgment on the abolition of slavery was never known.

Deeply affected by their brother's death, Angelina and Sarah busied themselves composing a memorial to Thomas. In this sketch they tried to convey the value and depth of their brother's convictions, as well as outlining his scholarly contributions.

It seemed as if life itself had stopped for Sarah and Angelina. Angelina's diary stopped after Edward Bettle's death, and with the death of Thomas, Sarah made the last entry in hers. It was as if they had broken all ties with the outside world. Sarah was forty-three. Angelina was thirty. Alone, disappointed, spinsters, it seemed as if that would be all for the sisters. Actually, their real life was only beginning.

6

New Beginnings

For a while after Thomas's death, Sarah and Angelina resigned themselves to the quiet, frustrating existence that life seemed to have destined them for. The future seemed too grim to think of. They were alone, with no real family left except each other, and even in their church and charity work things were not always as they would have liked them to be. And slavery, that old, ugly subject which had driven them from Charleston, and pursued them through their lives, was pursuing them even here. New winds were blowing, new ideas and solutions were reaching them, even in their secluded Quaker world.

At a Quaker meeting one day, Angelina tried to broach the subject among a group of fellow worshipers. "You would do well," one of them told her (frowning all the while at the thought of this brazen woman, who dared to occupy herself with such matters), "to leave the issue to wiser people." Charities, prayer meetings, household duties were enough for other women—why not for these Grimke' sisters?

But Angelina could not "leave the issue." She had heard, by now, of a new voice against slavery. In Boston a man by the name of William Lloyd Garrison had begun a weekly newspaper called *The Liberator,* which, he announced, would be dedicated to the immediate emancipation of all slaves. Garrison's paper had been banned in the South, and even in Philadelphia its radical message was frowned upon by many. Determined, Angelina became a faithful reader of *The Liberator.* It was a beginning, at least.

Sarah tried to join a local peace group, but to no avail. When she was told that Quakers did not join in groups with members of other sects, she withdrew quietly. But Angelina had a more independent disposition.

In 1835, Angelina began attending meetings of the Philadelphia Female Anti-Slavery Society. One night the society had a very special guest speaker, an abolitionist by the name of George Thompson. Sarah, her face narrowed with concern, watched as Angelina tied the ribbon on her grey bonnet. "But are you sure you should go?"

"Sarah," said Angelina suddenly, turning to face her elder sister, "you of all people should know my feelings on this matter. The abolitionists have principles which are our principles. How could I not go?"

"But the danger," began Sarah, "you know this man Thompson's reputation—the mobs, the riots wherever he appears. Can it be safe to go?"

But Angelina would not be dissuaded. "I must and I will go," she said, and that was that.

Too timid to accompany her sister, Sarah resigned herself to an uneasy wait for Angelina's return.

To Angelina's surprise, the meeting hall was packed—over a thousand people had come to hear Thompson speak. And as she listened to the British abolitionist, whom some said had been sent by "a group of little old ladies in Glasgow" to meddle in another country's affairs, it seemed as if a new light were dawning in her life. Here was someone else who felt as strongly as she did about the horrors of slavery. Perhaps there was hope, after all.

Her eyes were shining when she returned home. Enthusiastically she told Sarah of Thompson's argument for immediate emancipation, his tales of cruelty under the slavery system—cruelty which both the sisters had seen with their own eyes—his vigorous defense of his ideas when questioners from the floor tried to argue him down. "And I will," she told Sarah, "do all I can in the Anti-Slavery Society. Mr. Thompson says there is just as much need for women in the movement as for men."

"But Angelina—" began Sarah, her old doubts and memories of frustrated attempts rising to the fore. Sarah remembered her own disappointments, remembered the mob that had met Thomas when he tried to stand up for the Union. If even their beloved brother had failed, what could two women hope to accomplish? And besides, even in Philadelphia, it wasn't quite proper for women to engage in such activities.

"Proper or not, I will do it!" declared Angelina. And that was that.

Eagerly she scanned the newspapers for accounts of abolitionist activities, reading the speeches, book reviews and reports of meetings in Northern cities. Violence against abolitionists frequently filled the news. Angelina had expected a violent reaction in the South, but reports of disturbances throughout the North convinced her that even this was not the haven of open-mindedness she had once thought it to be.

In 1834 there had been riots in Philadelphia and New

York. State troops had been called out to end the race riots in New York. The Philadelphia violence was not ended until forty-five Negro homes had been destroyed and many persons injured. In Massachusetts a minister was stoned when he preached on emancipation. Angelina took special note of the fact that even respectable women were not immune from attack. A Quaker schoolteacher in Connecticut had dared to run a school for Negro children. As a result she was mobbed, jailed and eventually forced to abandon the effort.

Charleston had also made news in the summer of 1835. When a rumor was started that abolitionist literature had been shipped to the city and was being kept in the Charleston post office, an angry mob broke into the building, opened the mail sacks and burned the "incendiary literature" at a public bonfire. An effigy of William Lloyd Garrison was also burned. "Is there anywhere that men still have open minds?" Angelina asked herself.

George Thompson still encountered hostility wherever he traveled. Garrison's *Liberator* carried an editorial appealing to the public to rise up and condemn the violence which had threatened Thompson. Seeing a way to give support to these brave crusaders, Angelina wrote a private letter to Garrison, expressing her loyalty to his cause:

I can hardly express to thee the deep and solemn interest with which I have viewed the violent proceedings of the last few weeks. Although I expected opposition, I was not prepared for it so soon . . . I greatly feared abolitionists would be driven back. . . . I am grateful that you are ready to die rather than be driven back. The ground upon which you stand is holy:

never—never surrender it. If you surrender it, the hope of the slave is extinguished. . . . If persecution is the means which God has ordained for the accomplishment of this great end, EMANCIPATION; then . . . LET IT COME; for it is my deep, solemn deliberate conviction, that this is a cause worth dying for. . . .

Angelina hesitated several days before getting up enough courage to send the letter. Then she mailed it.

When Garrison received her letter, he was elated—here was a religious passion against slavery almost equal to his own. He immediately recognized the signer of the letter. Without asking Angelina's permission, Garrison published the letter in the next issue of *The Liberator,* introducing the writer as the sister of "the famed Thomas Grimke" and "a member of one of the South's finest families."

Garrison had predicted that Angelina's letter would arouse great interest. Sarah was afraid that the letter might cause undue pain to their family in Charleston; then one day a delegation of Quakers came to Angelina to protest her brash action.

"Angelina, we hope that you know the shame you have brought to your fellow Quakers," they began.

"Because I am opposed to slavery?" she asked in astonishment.

"No, you know what we mean. Because you have associated your name with that fanatical Garrison. Many of our brethren even fear for their lives. You know what people in this city think of the abolitionists. If we are associated with them, it could mean trouble for us."

"It is strange that men who work for right are now called fanatics," remarked Angelina in a biting tone.

"We will not argue with you," said one of the older

members. "We have only come to demand that you retract your letter. You must write to Garrison and withdraw it from his paper."

"I am sorry that I cannot comply with your wishes," replied Angelina, a bit offended at their rudeness. "None of you seem to understand that my letter was not a hasty act, conceived in a moment of emotion. That letter was the product of the entire span of my life, the logical conclusion toward which I have been moving all these years, the path which God has revealed to me."

The brethren saw, as many would see after them, that once Angelina Grimke' had made up her mind, there was little that could be said or done to stop her.

7

Angelina's Plea

Garrison used Angelina's letter for all that it was worth, reprinting it again in a pamphlet which included a poem by John Greenleaf Whittier. In October he brought out a special issue of *The Liberator* which contained enthusiastic reader reaction to the letter. Abolitionists throughout the country hailed it as a moving testament against slavery. Women's abolition and peace societies sent Angelina letters of support. Through no direct action of her own, she was thus thrust before the public as an active abolitionist.

But Angelina had not yet committed herself to full participation in the movement. All of this notoriety was new to her, and in reality she was still on the sidelines, reading about the riots, mobbings, charges and counter-charges. In the summer of 1835, a mob had broken up a meeting of the Boston Female Anti-Slavery Society, seizing Garrison and dragging him through the streets of Boston by a rope. His life had been spared only by the intervention of the mayor of Boston, who rescued him from the mob.

"What can I do?" Angelina asked herself. "What can a woman do to bring about change?" One answer was increased participation in the local women's antislavery society, and despite the condemnation of many of her fellow Quakers, she continued to work in the society. It was here that she met Lucretia Mott, a fellow Quakeress, mother of six and champion of many causes. Mrs. Mott led Philadelphia's Free Produce Movement, an attempt to protest slavery by refusing to buy any goods which were grown or manufactured using slaves. Although the boycott never really affected Southern trade, its importance lay in its symbolic expression of an abhorrence to slavery. For the first time, even Sarah became interested in this form of antislavery action, and she joined her sister in supporting the free produce concept.

Mrs. Grimké's daughters continued to correspond with their aging mother in Charleston. They begged her to give up her slaves, but their begging had little effect.

Meanwhile, a subtle change was occurring in their relationship with the Quakers. Angelina had become more sensitive to the racial prejudice in her midst, and one of the places where she saw racism in operation was, to her surprise, the Quaker meeting.

Through her work in the Female Anti-Slavery Society, she had met the pious and well-educated Sarah Douglass, a black woman who taught school in Philadelphia. This friendship increased her awareness of the error of Quaker prejudice. Sarah Douglass had been attending Quaker meetings for some time, but all Negroes were required to sit on a special "colored bench" which was placed at the back of the room apart from the white worshippers. This practice of racial segregation distressed Angelina and Sarah.

Their black friend told them about the time she had visited a Quaker meeting in New York. "As I entered the meetinghouse, a woman asked me, 'Are you coming to clean house?' " Sarah replied that she was a school teacher, not a maid. The lady expressed her astonishment and rushed off. Although Sarah attended worship services regularly, she had never been admitted to membership in the Philadelphia Quaker society. The reason had nothing to do with her religion; it was because of her color.

The Quaker's obvious prejudice against Sarah Douglass was more than the sisters could bear. Now Angelina read *The Liberator* with greater interest than she did the Quaker newspapers. But where would the sisters go if they finally broke with the Quakers? No single woman of that day could live alone and still be considered respectable. They would have to find other friends who would be willing to keep them.

Feelings of uselessness plagued Angelina. It was all right for Sarah to just drift along, busying herself with the Free Produce stores, but Angelina felt she had more to give. Other abolitionists had told her that her unique knowledge of slavery and her dedication to the cause should be shared with more people. How could she do this? Friends and duties in Philadelphia kept her out of full participation in the movement. Then one night Angelina heard "voices." The next morning she awoke with a joy and radiance such as she had not known for years. She was sure it was a divine revelation telling her what she should do.

"Sarah," Angelina announced excitedly over breakfast, "I have been shown the way that I should go. I will write an appeal to the women of the South, urging them to help overthrow slavery. Surely they will listen to one of their own—a Southerner and a woman. My appeal will reach the ears of those who have been closed to the words of the Northern abolitionists." Never standing in Angelina's way, Sarah gave her sister every encouragement. Angelina began at once and finished her *Appeal to the Christian Women of the Southern States* in only two weeks.

For the first time, a Southern woman was addressing her fellow Southern women on the evils of slavery. In simple, direct language, Angelina appealed to the women of the South to uphold the natural rights of the Negro. Did not the Declaration of Independence declare that all men were equal and that all men had natural rights to freedom? Using her knowledge of the Bible, Angelina refuted the biblical defense of slavery. She admitted that the Bible said the Hebrews had held slaves, but she showed how Hebrew servitude was more kind and just than Southern slavery. Unlike Hebrew slavery, Southern slavery robbed a slave of all his rights and all his dignity:

God never made a slave, *he made man upright, his back was* not *made to carry burdens, nor his neck to wear a yoke, and the man must be crushed within him, before* his *back can be* fitted *to the burden of perpetual slavery; and that his back is* not *fitted to it, is manifest by the insurrections that so often disturb the peace and security of slaveholding countries.*

Why, her readers might ask, appeal to them? They were only women who did not make the laws of the state. They had no vote, no political power.

I know you do not make the laws, but I also know that you are the wives and mothers, the sisters and daughters of those who do; and if you really suppose you can do nothing to overthrow slavery, you are greatly mistaken. . . . 1st You can read on this subject. 2nd You can pray over this subject. 3d You can speak on this subject. 4th You can act on this subject. . . . Speak to your relatives, friends, acquaintances, be not afraid . . . let your sentiments be known. . . . persuade your husband, father, brothers and sons that slavery is a crime against God and man.

Angelina urged her readers to free their own slaves, give them wages, and at least educate them so that they might have a chance to develop themselves.

As for Southern laws which forbid such practices, "wicked laws ought to be no barrier in the way of your duty. . . . If a law commands me to sin I will break it: if it calls me to suffer, I will let it take its course unresistingly." She called for petitions to state legislatures, disobedience of laws which perpetuated slavery, and a commitment on the part of Southern women to help abolish this evil in their midst.

The *Appeal* set forth, in simple, bold logic a plan of action for the women of the South. Angelina realized, from her own failures while she was in the South, that the *Appeal* would not have too great an effect upon Southern women. But she hoped that some would read it and take it to heart. Besides, the *Appeal* might provide fresh ammunition for Northern abolitionists. At any rate, she sent the finished manuscript off to the American Anti-Slavery Society in New York, with instructions to publish it with her name on the cover. "My family name is probably worth more than I am and will add weight to the argument," she reasoned.

The Anti-Slavery Society was elated. George Thompson wrote an introduction to the book and had it published in England, then the Society distributed it all over the North. But everyone was so enthusiastic over Angelina's work. Some of the Philadelphia Quakers were enraged.

Invitations came from all over New England, asking Angelina to lecture at Anti-Slavery Society meetings. She asked her Quaker meeting for permission to accept the invitations. They refused, but Angelina and Sarah decided to go anyway, with or without the blessings of the Quakers. They knew their work would embarrass the Quakers, since they could hardly expel the sisters for preaching something which Quakers were supposed to be in favor of.

In the fall of 1836 Angelina received an invitation from the Anti-Slavery Society of New York to come and work as an antislavery agent. Angelina and Sarah talked it over and decided to go.

8

The Lion

While Angelina and Sarah were preparing to depart for New York, a package containing copies of Angelina's new book reached the post office in Charleston. The postmaster opened the package, took a brief look at its contents, and then publicly burned the books. Charlestonians were enraged that one of their own number should so betray her homeland. It was whispered about town that if the Misses Grimké valued their lives, they should never return to the port city again. One afternoon the mayor of Charleston called upon Mrs. Grimké to inform her that should her daughters return to Charleston, he would be forced to imprison them and send them back on the first northbound boat. Sarah and Angelina would never again see their home.

Now a new city had come into their lives. New York—this energetic city made even Philadelphia look small. Here was the financial center of the North, a city where men played with railroads and factories, a city crowded with people from many nations who had come to seek their fortunes. The Grimkés arrived in October 1836. A few weeks later they were preparing to take part in the first "antislavery agents' convention."

The convention marked the beginning of a new level

of antislavery agitation. For the first time, agents were to be professionally trained on a large scale.

The brightest stars of abolitionism had come to the convention. Angelina and Sarah were thrilled to meet William Lloyd Garrison, crusading editor of *The Liberator.* Despite what they had read in the papers about Garrison's "fire-breathing fanaticism," they found him to be, "mild-mannered, soft-spoken, and gentlemanly."

"But you have yet to meet the real prophet of abolitionism," a friend told them.

"Who can that be if it is not Mr. Garrison?" asked Angelina.

"Theodore Weld," the friend answered, "the 'lion of the tribe of abolitionism.' Since Mr. Garrison converted Theodore Weld to the idea of immediate emancipation of slaves, Weld has traveled throughout the West, preaching and teaching against slavery."

"How successful has he been?" asked Sarah, still doubtful that any man could equal Garrison.

"Two years ago Weld almost single-handedly converted the entire student body of Lane Seminary to abolitionism, sending them out all over Ohio to convert the state. No man has suffered more attacks, mobbings and threats than Theodore Weld. We abolitionists regard that as a measure of success. Although he is a strict pacifist who would never lift a hand against his fellowman, there are stories of how he has stilled even the most hostile mobs, just by the strength of his convictions."

"We will be anxious to meet this famed Mr. Weld," said Angelina.

"You will not have long to wait. He will be leading the training sessions for the new anti-slavery agents."

The next day they met "the lion." Angelina recorded her first sight of Weld in a letter to one of her friends in Philadelphia:

A tall and lanky man walked to the center of the convention hall stage. Even from where I was sitting I could see that his face bore the scars of his hazardous career. But at first sight, there was nothing remarkable in his appearance. He had a rough and dishelveled look and I wondered whether he was really as great as I had heard. But as soon as his countenance became animated by speaking, I found it was one which portrayed the noblest qualities of the heart and head beaming with intelligence, benevolence, and frankness.

Few men had Weld's speaking ability. He opened the first training session with a talk on the rights of man. "I was deeply moved," exclaimed Sarah. "I never heard so grand and beautiful an exposition of the dignity of man."

But the high point for the sisters came at the end of the meeting, when Garrison led Angelina and Sarah down to the front of the hall and introduced them to Weld, who greeted them as, "my dear sisters." They were surprised to know that, even in the West, Weld had heard of their names.

"How did you first become interested in abolitionism, Mr. Weld?" asked Angelina, trying to make conversation.

"Probably in much the same way that you two did," Weld replied. "During my childhood in Connecticut, I saw my classmates and teacher ridicule the only Negro boy in my class. Out of pity for the boy, I asked for permission to sit next to him each day. Thereafter the

persecution stopped. I have been an abolitionist ever since."

Although Weld's voice had been impaired by years of strenuous outdoor speaking, he did not spare it during the convention. Many days he spoke for eight or ten hours. As the training period progressed, Weld raised and refuted every possible argument against abolition. He drew on his vast personal experience, lecturing agents on how to handle mobs, how to form anti-slavery societies, what books to suggest to interested persons.

The new agents listened intently. Soon they would be put to the test. Just how great a test it might be was indicated in the testimony of one agent, who told how his trunk had been broken into in Nashville, Tennessee. When a few antislavery pamphlets were found, he had been sentenced to be whipped publicly in the town square, before the most prominent ministers of Nashville.

The meetings adjourned for the last time on November 27, after a month of instruction, and the new agents departed for their assignments. For the first time in their lives Angelina and Sarah felt as if they were members of a group of like-minded people.

The sisters began by giving a series of "parlor talks" to women in private homes in New York. The response was so great that no parlor was large enough to hold them. A local Baptist minister volunteered the use of his church for their lectures, but some of the abolitionist leaders had second thoughts. It was one thing for the sisters to speak in private homes and quite another thing to open their talks to the public. The Bible clearly stated that women should not speak in public. Did not the Apostle Paul say, "I do not allow a woman to teach, nor to usurp authority over a man, but rather to be in silence"?

Weld encouraged them to go ahead. "I deplore customs which keep women from exercising their God-given abilities and talents," he declared. His support strengthened Sarah and Angelina, and they decided to continue. Though they were timid and unsure of themselves at first, their zeal gave them courage. Night after night, their speaking ability improved and the crowds grew. Sarah usually spoke on the moral and theological questions, while Angelina talked about anti-slavery organization and political strategy.

The new experiences refreshed Sarah. At last she had found, along with her sister, a suitable outlet for her energies. Late in 1836 she tried her hand at writing. The result was Sarah's *Epistle to the Clergy of the Southern States,* an address to the clergymen of the South on the sin of slavery. Though Sarah's writing style was not as clear as her sister's, she nevertheless showed a mastery of Christian arguments against slavery.

The sisters were attracting national attention. That same year a letter appeared in a New Haven, Connecticut, newspaper. The writer of the letter told them to "quit bothering the North with your abolitionist speeches. What," he asked, "would you ladies have Northerners do?" Sarah and Angelina had a ready response to the question.

In their reply, they declared "Southern slavery could never have existed without Northern support. Northern states have bowed to Southern demands to extend slavery into the new Western territories. They return fugitive slaves to their Southern masters. Their pulpits and political rostrums are silent on the evil. Northern bankers support Southern slave plantations." In addition, they declared that Northern racial prejudice was "grinding the colored man to dust in our free states," and "making life miserable for those few Negroes who live in Northern cities."

This Southern attack on Yankee racism was something new, and most Yankees did not like it one bit. "Stick to attacks on Southern slavery," their abolitionist friends advised them, "and avoid discussions about the lesser evil of Northern racial prejudice." But Angelina and Sarah refused. They were convinced that slavery would never be conquered as long as white people in the North continued to look upon black people as inferiors.

Theodore Weld supported the sisters. "You can make a unique contribution to the movement," he said. But Sarah and Angelina had found once again that even among abolitionists it was easier to attack other men's sins than to have one's own sins exposed.

In the summer of 1837 they traveled to New York for the convention of American Anti-Slavery Women. Here the sisters continued to attack Northern racial prejudice as the basis for Southern slavery. "It is fine for many of you to talk about the Negro in the abstract, as long as he is removed from you," Angelina charged, "but quite another thing to accept him as your equal."

And here the Grimke' sisters introduced yet another bold new concept into the abolitionist movement. Angelina declared, "Women, because of their sex, have been held back and denied their natural rights for centuries. Women ought to feel a peculiar sympathy in the colored man's wrong, for, like him, she has been accused of mental inferiority, and denied the privileges of a liberal education. If we do not act in this matter and exercise our natural right to speak out against this evil, then may *we* well be termed the white slaves of the North, for like our brethren in bonds, we must seal our lips in silence and despair."

The Grimke' sisters had thereby identified the struggles for racial and female equality. Some criticized them for getting "sidetracked," for attacking "irrelevant" issues. But for most of the women who heard them speak that day, Sarah and Angelina had infused a new breath of hope into the common struggle for human rights. Refusing to be mere spokesmen for the cause or to let others take the lead, the Grimke's had now become shapers of events and leaders in yet another area of injustice.

9

A Voice for Women

Sarah and Angelina had been invited to Boston. Here, less than a century before, revolutionaries had withstood the king's Redcoats, held the world's most famous "tea party" and, in a small village only a few miles away, fired the "shot heard 'round the world." True to its revolutionary heritage, Boston had once again become a center of controversy, for it was now a stronghold of abolitionism.

From Boston Garrison published the fiery *Liberator.* Women's abolitionist groups met all over the city, circulating petitions to Congress, collecting money for anti-slavery campaigns, and hosting traveling antislavery agents like the Grimkes. Ironically, conservatives in other parts of the nation often compared Boston to Charleston, its opposite pole on the slavery question. Both cities had become known as hotbeds of "radicals, rabble rousers, and rebels" who could be counted on to take the opposite extremes on nearly every issue.

"At last," Angelina declared, "we have found a receptive city in which abolitionists are given a fair hearing." More amazing still, "even Quakers here are vigorous abolitionists." There also seemed to be less prejudice against the idea of women who spoke in public. For the first time the sisters addressed mixed audiences of men and women—a novelty for that day. Often as many as a thousand people came to hear these odd little women from South Carolina who were assaulting Yankeedom with their abolitionism. During their first twenty-three weeks in New England they spoke to over 40,000 people at meetings in sixty-seven towns.

A few days after their arrival, Sarah and Angelina accompanied William Lloyd Garrison on a visit to John Quincy Adams, former President of the United States, now a member of the House of Representatives. Adams had become known as a friend of the abolitionists. He was presently holding forth in Congress against Southerners (led by John C. Calhoun) who were attempting to keep the abolitionists from swamping Congress with antislavery petitions. By refusing to receive the petitions, Southerners hoped to stifle discussion on the volatile issue. Though Adams had refused to support the abolitionists publicly, he stubbornly defended their right to send their petitions to Congress, saying that it was a matter of free speech.

"We have come to you to ask you for a commitment to greater public support of abolitionism," Garrison told Adams.

"You are our chief hope in Congress," added Angelina.

"Politics is a game of compromise," Adams began. "If I were to openly identify myself with your cause, I should end my usefulness to you. No, I can best serve you by upholding your right to petition Congress, rather than by speaking out openly in behalf of your cause."

The Grimke's were greatly disappointed. They knew little of compromise. "It is a simple matter of right or wrong to us," said Angelina. "Either you are completely for us, Mr. Adams, or you are against us."

Adams listened to this little lecture with patience. He had seen reformers before and felt that they sometimes were hindered by their own zeal for their cause.

"We left the meeting sick at heart of political morality," Sarah reported to a friend.

Despite the Grimkes' joy at the "openness of Boston," not all Bostonians were in sympathy with abolitionists. As their cause won more adherents, it became more feared. Hearing Southern threats in Congress, many were convinced that the abolitionists were needlessly stirring up a hornet's nest of sectional strife, and Garrison's continual accusations and condemnations did nothing to cool things down. *The Liberator* attacked the Constitution, the President, Congress, clergymen, businessmen and anyone else who raised even a mild objection to abolitionism.

Even in New England, abolitionists were finding more pulpits and lecture halls closed to them. The Congregationalist ministers of Boston had refused to read notices of abolitionist meetings from their pulpits. Congregationalists in Connecticut had passed resolutions forbidding "traveling agents" from using their churches without consent of the pastors. Unable to find a single church or meeting hall open to them, Boston abolitionists were forced to hold their 1837 convention in a converted stable.

As for Sarah and Angelina, opposition strengthened their dedication. In the middle of a lecture in Amesbury, Massachusetts, Angelina was interrupted by two young men who challenged her from the floor.

"We have been in the South," one of the young men

shouted, "and we have found that the condition of the slaves is not bad at all. They have plenty to eat, a place to sleep, someone to worry about them. I doubt that the slaves of the South are as bad off as the poor farm laborers and mill workers in the North."

The audience asked Angelina for a reply. She returned the next night to debate the issue. As the debate opened in a packed meetinghouse, one of their opponents gave the usual biblical proslavery argument. He was no match for Angelina, who was an expert on the Bible and on slavery. After demolishing his argument she turned to a comparison of Northern workers and Southern slaves.

"While I admit that some Northern workers labor under terrible conditions, and while I especially deplore the fact that women do the same work in factories but get less pay for it, the Northern worker is free, while the slave is not. White workers can improve themselves, advance in status, move around to better jobs. The slave has none of these freedoms. He dies in the same status in which he was born. The white worker has self-respect, while the slave remains in a perpetually degraded condition."

Angelina's triumph was complete. The next day some newspapers declared themselves scandalized by the "spectacle of a woman daring to debate men in public." But in many cities Angelina's victory was praised as a "step forward for abolitionism and a credit to the talents of women."

The sisters realized that too often the real obstacle to their message was not the message itself, but the fact that it was being delivered by a woman.

It was Catherine Beecher, female educator and

founder of the Hartford Female Seminary (which Angelina had once tried to attend), who finally drew the sisters into a heated debate over women's rights. Early in 1837 Miss Beecher had published an essay which criticized abolitionists and their attempts to organize women into political pressure groups. She admitted that her essay was a direct reply to Angelina's *Appeal.* The Grimke's realized that they had met a formidable opponent. Miss Beecher defended the Colonization Society's plan for gradual emancipation and removal of slaves to Africa. She opposed the practice of women petitioning Congress, saying, "Men are the proper persons to make appeals to the rulers whom they appoint."

Angelina's reply to Miss Beecher was in the form of a series of letters in *The Liberator.* Easily she refuted the old colonization arguments; she had been through all that before with Thomas. By planning to ship all Negroes back to Africa, Angelina charged that Miss Beecher had bowed to racial prejudice: "Surely you never want to get rid of people whom you *love.* . . . It is because I love the colored Americans, that I want them to stay in this country; and in order to make it a happy home to them, I am trying to talk down, and write down and live down, this horrible prejudice. Sending a few to Africa cannot destroy it. No—we must dig up the weed by the roots out of each of our hearts." How, she asked, could anyone be a "gradualist" in the face of an evil like slavery?

The colonization issue having been taken care of, Angelina moved into what she considered to be the most damaging aspect of Miss Beecher's essay, women's rights. She was disgusted at her opponent's suggestion that women should stay home in the kitchen and nursery and let the world be run by men. Evidently this "pioneer of female education" had a limited idea of what women were supposed to do with that education.

Since women have been denied their right to vote, hold property or make a contract, would they also be denied the right to petition? Would they even be denied their right to speak? In Angelina's mind, Catherine Beecher had betrayed her sisters. Leaving no doubt as to her own position, Angelina demanded rights equal to those of men: "I believe it is woman's right to have a voice in all the laws by which she is governed, whether in Church or State: and that the present arrangements of society, on these points, are a *violation of human rights.*"

Finally, linking the cause of slaves with that of women, she described both as a common struggle for democracy: "The discussion of the rights of the slave has opened the ways for the discussion of other rights, and the ultimate result will most certainly be the breaking of *every* yoke, the letting the oppressed of every grade and description go free, an emancipation far more glorious than any the world has yet seen."

Angelina's advocacy of women's rights did not go unnoticed. In July 1837 the Congregational churches of Massachusetts passed a resolution which, while not mentioning any names, accused certain "female agitators" of spreading dissension and strife among the churches and bringing "shame and dishonor" to their "fair sex." Everyone knew it was the Grimke' sisters to whom the resolution was addressed.

It was soon apparent that Sarah and Angelina were

not alone in their yearning for equal rights. All over New England women came to their defense, and they received invitations to speak to hundreds of women's groups. Wherever they spoke, women walked miles, frequently against the orders of their husbands, to hear them. When male hecklers attempted to break up a lecture, local women rushed to their defense and ordered the men to leave. The public had linked them with the women's rights issue and in so doing had linked the cause of slaves with that of women. Many thought the Grimkes were better feminists than they were abolitionists.

In February 1838 Angelina was invited to speak before a committee of the Massachusetts legislature. She was to present an antislavery petition signed by 20,000 women. Never before had a woman been allowed to speak before such an august gathering.

At noon on February 21 a crowd began gathering at the Massachusetts State House. By two o'clock the legislators had to climb over the seats in order to get to their places. The galleries were so packed that some feared that they would collapse. Angelina needed the greatest courage in order to stand before the group. Would they give her a fair hearing? Would she be heard in such a packed room?

A little after two o'clock she rose to speak. After presenting the stack of petitions to the chairman, she said, "These petitions relate to the solemn subject of slavery. . . . And because it is a political subject, it has often been said that women had nothing to do with it. Are we aliens, because we are mothers, wives and daughters of a mighty people? Have women *no* country—no interests staked in public weal—no liabilities in common peril—no partnership in a nation's guilt and shame?"

She was interrupted by hisses from the rear of the room and the chairman asked her to stop. The heckling continued for a few more minutes, until the crowd made it clear that they wished to hear more from Miss Grimké. Soon she had captured the audience with her skillful oratory:

"I stand before you as a Southerner, exiled from the land of my birth by the sound of the lash and the piteous cry of the slave. I stand before you as a repentent slaveholder. . . . as a moral being I feel that I owe it to the suffering slave and to the deluded master, to my country and to the world to do all that I can to overturn a system of complicated crimes, built upon the broken hearts and prostrate bodies of my countrymen in chains and cemented by the blood, sweat and tears of my sisters in bonds."

Her audience was visibly moved. After two hours the meeting adjourned. It was a truly significant event in the history of abolitionism and women's rights, but not everyone was enthusiastic about Angelina's performance. One newspaper reported that she "appeared not at all abashed in exhibiting herself in a position so unsuitable to her sex, totally disregarding the doctrine of St. Paul, who says 'Is it not a shame for a woman to speak in public?' " Another Boston newspaper cuttingly remarked, "It is doubtful whether any of the South Carolina lords of creation will ever seek the heart and hand of their great orator in marriage."

But there was some public support. Most abolitionists were jubilant. From as far away as Detroit an editorial

declared, "Miss Grimke', a pretty Quakeress . . . is a woman of splendid eloquence and has made me 19/20 of an abolitionist."

Angelina could not help thinking to herself, "We abolition women are turning the world upside down."

All of this female agitation was viewed with mixed emotions by some abolitionists, who heard comments that they were "nothing but a bunch of discontented old maids." Some, like Theodore Weld, supported equality for women. But Weld was afraid that the Grimke's had sidetracked many female abolitionists from the main cause of slavery. He respectfully asked the sisters to "talk less about women's rights and more about the ending of slavery." After all, was not abolition the most pressing issue?

"We admit the primacy of abolition of slavery," Angelina wrote to Weld. "But how," she asked, "do you suppose that we are to accomplish the mission of freeing the slaves when we are denied the right to speak, to petition, to publish, to debate? If we are to do the cause of abolition any good, our right to full participation must be established."

The debate with Weld ended in a compromise. The sisters agreed to end public agitation on women's rights. "But we will maintain our firm commitment to women's rights," they pledged, "and will defend them whenever challenged." They admitted that ending slavery was the first order of business. As Angelina said, "the cause of the Negro is the common cause of women; until he gets his rights, we shall never have ours."

10

Love and Riots

Although Weld had disappointed Sarah and Angelina by his failure to support their campaign for women's rights, their admiration for him remained strong. For several months they conducted a lively exchange of letters with Weld over the issue. They debated questions of theory, strategy and practical measures for bringing about change. The sisters relied upon Weld's advice in nearly everything they undertook. Soon it became clear, at least to Angelina, that the correspondence with Weld was becoming more personal. Something more than a debate over abolitionist strategy was at stake.

Since they had first met him at the antislavery agents' convention, Weld had been their guiding light. Although he was an exceedingly modest man who shunned personal glory, stories of his exciting life were part of abolitionist lore. They told of his strength and vitality, of his amazing feats. At fourteen Weld had taken complete charge of his father's hundred-acre farm. A few years later he had traveled throughout the Northeast lecturing on the "science of mnemonics," or memory training. In his early twenties, Weld had been converted at a revival; afterwards he had become a traveling evangelist, developing his extraordinary abilities for organization and public speaking. He was known to be one of the nation's best public speakers. In addition, Weld had done everything from shipping aboard a whaler to teaching in college.

One February, while traveling in Ohio, he had been almost drowned in a flood-swollen creek. His coach overturned in the raging current, Weld had become tangled in the reins, and was dragged down again and again under the freezing waters. He was swept down the creek, knocked against rocks, and nearly drowned before he grabbed an old tree stump protruding into the stream. By a fortunate coincidence, some men who happened to live in a cabin nearby—the only cabin along the creek for several miles—had heard his cries and rescued him from the icy waters. The rescue seemed like an act of God to Weld, and from that time on he vowed to dedicate his life to the service of God. His dedication took the form of a crusade against slavery.

Now thirty-five, his voice exhausted and reduced to a whisper by countless sermons and lectures on abolitionism, Weld was working in the New York office of the American Anti-Slavery Society. He bore the scars of a hard-earned reputation as "the most mobbed man in the United States." Tall, thin and slouched, with an uncut beard and scuffed boots, the famous crusader was still a commanding figure, appearing strong and fierce to those who met him. Living in a small, unheated room, Weld took no pay for his labors. He lived, ate and went to church only with black people, setting an example of brotherhood for other abolitionists.

It was well known that Theodore Weld had vowed never to marry until slavery had been abolished. He had always thought that marriage would impede his work.

Sarah and Angelina had heard of Weld's vow but thought little of it. They had no thought of becoming intimate with him. Weld had always gone out of his way to remain cool and aloof toward all women.

But little touches of intimacy crept into their correspondence. Angelina often inquired about his health. "Do you eat well?" she would ask. "Are you overworking? Do you have a warm office in which to work?" Sometimes she gently teased him for his poor handwriting—"scratchifications," as she called it. Weld tried to remain cool to Angelina's friendliness. He continued to speak of the Grimke's as "respected fellow agents," and not as close friends.

Late in November 1837, a visiting Massachusetts abolitionist called upon Weld to tell him that Angelina was seriously ill. Excessive overwork during her last speaking tour had impaired her health and it was feared that her lungs were permanently damaged. Weld was visibly upset. He pleaded with the sisters to discontinue their public speaking and to give themselves a much-needed rest.

"I entreat you as a brother," he wrote, "to save yourselves for the slave, for human rights, for woman's rights, and for the coming of Jesus Christ."

Sarah replied that Angelina was making a gradual recovery. Weld expressed relief. During her recuperation, Angelina and Weld worked together to bring out another edition of her *Appeal.* There was a more personal tone to their letters now. Weld was still careful, but Angelina shared even more of her intimate thoughts with him.

Then one day a special letter came, marked on the

outside of the envelope, in bold letters, PRIVATE. Angelina pondered. What could it mean? Could this be a rebuff from Weld? Would he tell her to mind her own business and keep her thoughts on her work? When she read the letter, she was struck with amazement. Weld had made a confession:

I know it will surprise and even amaze you, Angelina, when I say to you, that for a long time you have had my whole heart. . . . *Your letter to Wm. Lloyd Garrison formed an era in my feelings and a crisis in my history that drew my spirit toward yours by irrepressible affinities. I read it over and over. . . . I have been forced to tell you these things even though I know that you probably have no tender feelings for me.*

No feelings for him! Angelina could hardly believe her eyes. Had he been so insensitive to the subtle hints of her love? But then she realized that she was dealing with a man unskilled in the art of courtship. Quickly she answered his letter, assuring him of her strong feelings for him.

There followed a curious exchange of letters in which each confessed his or her faults. "I am full of pride," wrote Weld, adding that he had a bad temper and was prone to forgetfulness. The list of faults grew: "I have a woeful lack of education. The sum total of my acquired knowledge is about equal to that of the learned pig!"

Angelina in turn confessed her faults—"selfishness, impatience, irritability. But why," she asked, "should any of our faults stand in the way of our deep love? Love overlooks the minor faults and helps correct the larger ones."

After a few weeks of this, Weld at last admitted that

his thoughts had turned to marriage. He asked Angelina to be his wife saying:

We marry, Angelina . . . to do and dare, together to toil and testify and suffer, to keep ourselves unspotted from the world, to live a life of faith, rejoicing always to bear one another's burden, looking not each on his own things but each on the things of the other, in honor preferring one another and happy beyond expression."

One major obstacle stood in the way of a public announcement of their engagement. What would become of Sarah?

Anticipating the problem, she went to the couple on her own. "You must not worry about me," she assured them. "Angelina, you must lead your own life. There are friends that I can live with, and I would not stand in the way of your happiness for anything."

But Weld would not allow Sarah to leave. "I know enough about you two to know that you could not live apart from one another. I insist that you come to live with us, Sarah. There is much for us to do, and we can do it best if we stay together."

Sarah knew it might not be easy for her to adjust to life with a married couple, but what else was left for her? What kind of life could she lead by herself? So she accepted Theodore Weld's offer, "I guess I will be the typical old maid sister," she said to herself with a sigh.

The couple encountered mixed reactions from their fellow abolitionists. Most of their friends reacted to the news with sincere pleasure. Some of Angelina's friends were upset, feeling that marriage would end her public life. On the other hand, some of Weld's friends rudely questioned, "how any man could ever marry so strong-minded a woman as Angelina Grimké," but most of them agreed with the poet Whittier, who believed that Weld's marriage to Angelina was "the best thing a man could do."

Wedding invitations went out for May 14, 1838, inviting about eighty friends. True to their unorthodox natures, Angelina and Weld planned their wedding as a thoroughly unorthodox affair. Local society was scandalized when it learned that both blacks and whites had been invited. Like nearly everything else in their lives, the wedding was to be a symbolic statement of the bride and groom's convictions. A Negro baker made a wedding cake using only "free" sugar (produced by free labor); rather than have a formal ceremony, Angelina and Theodore decided simply to compose their own thoughts at the wedding and let those who attended sign a document attesting to the marriage.

On the anticipated day the pillars of abolitionism gathered in Philadelphia to see America's most mobbed man united in marriage to America's most talked-about woman. William Lloyd Garrison was there, taking credit for the whole affair. "Was it not I who introduced the two?" he asked.

Sarah Douglass was an honored guest. In Angelina's words, her presence "bore our testimony against the horrible prejudice against colored persons." Although Mrs. Grimke' could not attend, sister Anna was there, shocked speechless at the sight of all these "fanatics" under one roof. "What a motley crew did you assemble to witness the solemn scene," her mother commented when Angelina wrote her about the wedding.

The bride and groom appeared, simply dressed, and spoke to one another in "such words as the Lord gave them at the moment." Weld took the occasion to denounce, "laws which unrightfully gave the husband authority over the wife," and both black and white ministers offered brief prayers. Garrison read the marriage certificate and passed it around for all to sign. Thus Angelina Grimke' and Theodore Weld were married, using their wedding as a public testimony to their beliefs.

If anyone had thought that marriage would interfere with the public careers of the two abolitionists, they soon found that they were mistaken. The bride and groom had busied themselves with abolitionist activities right up to the wedding, and one day after their marriage they were back at work. That same week there was to be a national convention of antislavery women in Philadelphia's Pennsylvania Hall.

Pennsylvania Hall had just been dedicated. When Philadelphia reformers had found that many of the city's lecture halls were closed to them, they had decided to build their own. Pennsylvania Hall, erected by the contributions of hundreds of reformers and abolitionists, now stood as a symbol of free speech and social reform.

Many Philadelphians did not look with pleasure upon this "gathering place of radicals," and certain hostile elements in the city had openly declared that they intended to stop the women's convention from meeting. Ugly rumors had circulated through the town that the building was to be used for "immoral purposes," and that white women and black men had been seen strolling arm in arm into the hall on the opening day of the convention.

Yet the women remained firm in their determination to hold their convention. During the first session, as

Angelina Weld, bride of only two days, spoke to the group, a hostile mob gathered outside. Stones crashed through one of the windows, shattering glass on the audience. Angelina continued to speak, with a calm assurance which gave the women courage:

"What is a mob?" she asked. "What would the breaking of every window be? Any evidence that *we are* wrong or that slavery is a good and wholesome institution? What if that mob should now burst in upon us, break up our meeting and commit violence on our persons—would this be anything compared with what the slaves endure?" The clamor outside continued, but Angelina spoke for over an hour. Her audience stayed to hear her; the mob had failed to silence these dedicated women.

The next day the mayor of Philadelphia requested that the abolitionists keep Negro women from attending the meetings. Otherwise, he said, he and the chief of police might not be able to protect them. Lucretia Mott, long a dedicated Philadelphia abolitionist, led the group in refusing the mayor's request. The women were determined not to yield to mob intimidation.

But that night, when the abolitionists departed after their meeting, a dense crowd had gathered outside the hall. The crowd grew larger and more unruly; finally the mob surged forward, breaking down doors and rushing into the empty building. They kindled a fire with abolitionist records and literature. By the time the mayor and police arrived on the scene, Pennsylvania Hall was engulfed in flames. In a few hours the abolitionists' symbol of free speech was reduced to ashes. The crowd cheered and dispersed. The next night pro-slavery mobs even burned the Quaker orphanage for

Negro children and destroyed many Negro homes.

All across the nation newspapers condemned Philadelphia's mob violence, pointing to the "City of Brotherly Love" as a center of racial strife. But the condemnations were usually tempered with charges that the abolitionists had incited the riots with their "repulsive doctrines." The victims were blamed for the crime.

Determined to show the world that they would not be deterred from their course, the abolitionist women met again the morning after the fire, this time in a Philadelphia schoolroom. Speaking to the group, Sarah declared that the mob action demonstrated "that Northern racism is the bulwark of Southern slavery." Then she offered a resolution, calling upon abolitionists to identify themselves with "these oppressed Americans, by sitting with them in places of worship, by appearing with them in our streets, by giving them our countenance in steamboats and stages, by visiting them at their homes and encouraging them to visit us, receiving them as we do our white fellow citizens." The resolution passed unanimously.

11

The Quiet Life

When the convention adjourned, the Welds and Sarah Grimke' returned to their little cottage overlooking the Hudson River for a much-deserved rest. Sarah was now forty-six years old. Angelina was thirty-three. For the first time, the two sisters busied themselves with homemaking, while Weld looked on with amusement as Angelina burned the baked apples and undercooked the vegetables. Sarah, now living the role of the spinster sister, declared, "I am far more proud of my homemade bread than I have been of my anti-slavery lectures."

Angelina and Sarah had always been susceptible to strange new fads and theories; now they came under the influence of Sylvester Graham's ideas. Remembered today only as the originator of "Graham crackers," he had developed a Spartan diet which he advocated as being not only "most conducive to health" but also "an emancipation of woman from the toils of the kitchen." Following Graham's diet, the sisters cooked hot food only once a week, refrained from eating meat and served mostly uncooked fruit or cereal. Amazingly, they claimed that they were healthier than ever before.

For Angelina, marriage led to an increasing warmth with her mother. Now that her daughter was engaged in more orthodox activities, Mrs. Grimke' wrote often, giving motherly advice on keeping house and reporting family gossip. She sent them homemade pickles and a pair of socks for Weld, with the remark that he should return them if he had any reservations about wearing clothing made from slave-grown cotton. Her daughters continued to badger Mrs. Grimke' on the slavery issue, but pride and custom would not let her yield to their ideas.

The respite on the Hudson was short. The three reformers had too much energy to rest for long, and Weld had a brilliant idea for a new project. Nearly every book on abolition had been criticized for presenting a one-sided, uninformed, prejudiced view of slavery. Why not write a book about the cruelties of slavery based solely on the testimony of slaveholders themselves? Weld proposed to accomplish this by obtaining the testimonies of Southern abolitionists (what few there were), by using court records of trials involving slaves, and by collecting articles and editorials from Southern newspapers.

It was an ingenious approach. Weld wanted to be as honest as possible, and he made every effort to verify the first-hand accounts he collected on the brutality of slavery. But the most important part of his study was the collection of information from Southern newspapers. All that winter he, Angelina, and Sarah read and clipped thousands of papers. They collected advertisements for runaway slaves which described their physical characteristics–scars, whipmarks, brandings, iron collars, cropped ears, etc. Accounts of the punishments inflicted on blacks convicted of crime, together with state laws which showed the total lack of legal rights for blacks, all provided a true and horrifying picture of slavery. Then Weld investigated the housing and feeding of slaves, comparing their poor diet to that of the armed forces of several foreign countries. He also collected data on their medical care and work loads.

As Weld recalled,

> *After the work was finished we were curious to know how many newspapers had been examined. So we went up to our attic and took an inventory of bundles. When our count had reached* twenty thousand *newspapers, we said: "There, let that suffice." Though the book had in it many thousand facts thus authenticated by the slave-holders themselves, yet it contained but a tiny fraction of the nameless atrocities gathered from the papers examined.*

The final result was a devastating indictment of the slave system.

Angelina and Sarah then wrote short personal accounts of their own experiences in the South. Once again the sisters were forced to relive all the painful sights and sounds of the cruelties which they had witnessed. "When one considers," they wrote, "the fact that we had an opportunity to observe only the treatment of house servants, who were treated better than field hands, as well as the fact of our sheltered lives while in Charleston, it proves that the number of incidents which we witnessed must have been typical rather than extraordinary."

The finished work, *American Slavery As It Is*, was printed in 1839. It soon sold more copies than any other antislavery pamphlet ever written and was circulated widely in Britain; it became one of the most powerful weapons of the abolitionists. Harriet Beecher Stowe said later that she slept with the book under her pillow every night, in order to absorb all of its contents before writing her famous *Uncle Tom's Cabin.*

Reliving all the painful memories of their childhood had not been easy for Angelina and Sarah, and they were exhausted from the work. During the summer, while they were resting from the long task of preparing the book, they received word, through their sister Anna, that Mrs. Grimke' had died in Charleston after a long illness. Her death came as a blow to her exiled daughters. Of all the Grimke' family, their mother had been the most tolerant of her rebellious offspring. "At least," Anna spitefully remarked, "Mother was spared the bitter cup of your last infamous publication."

As busy housewives, Angelina and Sarah had less time to devote to abolitionist leadership. Although they made no major speeches after the Philadelphia convention, they devoted every spare moment to helping the abolitionist cause in any way they could. They continued to solicit signatures for petitions to Congress, and together they canvassed the area around their home. The people of this rural area seemed less inclined toward abolition than city dwellers.

Sarah trudged from house to house, explaining abolitionism and asking people to sign her petitions. Sometimes it was discouraging work.

"I'd rather see all the slaves shot than liberated," one woman told her. "All you are doing is leading us into war with the South."

Before another neighbor slammed her door in Sarah's face, she declared, "The only petition I will sign is one to ship all of you fanatics back to Africa with the niggers. Why don't you stay home with your family like you're supposed to?"

Throughout the nation similar resistance was encountered wherever petitions were circulated. But the campaign also accomplished worthwhile results. By calling at individual homes, abolitionists had an opportunity to explain their position personally.

Each time an antislavery petition was sent to Washington, it provoked renewed debate on the slavery issue. When Southern Congressmen tried to block the petitions, men like John Quincy Adams would rise to the defense of the petitioner's right to be heard. The Southerners knew that this constant flood was damaging to their position. By April 1838 the bundles of abolitionist petitions which had been presented at that Congressional session filled a large room closely packed all the way to the ceiling. It was estimated that their number ran into the millions.

In addition to petitioning Congress, abolitionists also started examining political candidates for local elections to see how they stood on the slavery issue. After 1840 few men could be elected for office in the North who were not at least mildly sympathetic toward the abolitionists. By 1837 there were over 1,000 local abolitionist societies, with a total membership in excess of 100,000. Abolitionism was now a truly significant movement.

Yet even as the movement achieved success, it was torn by internal controversy. William Lloyd Garrison and his followers around Boston had grown more radical, attaching all sorts of unrelated and volatile issues to the abolitionist cause. Soon Garrison's followers were angering other abolitionists with their outright denunciations of government—any government—and their refusal to work within the political system because of its "impurity." Once again Weld urged them to stick to the central issue of abolition and leave their radical political and social views out of it. Garrison denounced Weld as a "compromising conservative."

Soon the entire movement was split between such radicals and the "conservatives" like Weld and the Grimke's, who still believed that moral and political persuasion were the best means to bring about change. Angelina, Sarah and Weld tried to stay out of the controversy, but they looked on sadly as Garrison led his group in tearing apart the movement.

By the end of 1840 the national abolitionist society had split in two, and both factions were weakened by the battle. For the Welds, who had friends on both sides of the controversy, the division was a personal tragedy. Rather than take sides in the feud the three of them withdrew from national abolitionist activity. An era had ended for them.

In spite of this disappointment, new interests had come to the Weld household. In December 1839 Angelina gave birth to a baby boy. The new arrival was named Charles Stewart in honor of Weld's abolitionist friend.

At first the baby was kept on a rigid Grahamite diet, strictly limiting the amount of milk he was given. Despite the health claims of this diet, Charles seemed to cry a great deal. When Angelina went away for a few days, Sarah tried feeding the baby as much milk as he wanted. He immediately improved, becoming a happy and contented child. The sisters had learned that Mr.

Graham's theories on infant feeding were not infallible.

Due to the split in the national antislavery society, Weld's already meager salary of $1,000 a year was reduced to $800. By this time Sarah and Angelina's inheritance had dwindled, and they found that they were on the verge of a serious financial situation. In order to save money, the Welds decided to move to a little farm in Belleville, New Jersey, where they could raise their own food.

In January 1841 Angelina gave birth to another son. They named him Theodore. While this second birth so soon after the first one had weakened Angelina's health, it was a great joy to her. "As the mother of two children," she told Sarah, "I can answer all of those who have said I would never make a suitable wife or mother." She had proved that a woman could be an active writer, lecturer and organizer and still fill the traditional roles of wife and mother.

But not everyone felt that Angelina had mastered both roles. William Lloyd Garrison, bitter toward Weld and the sisters because they had failed to support him in the recent controversy, accused them of losing interest in abolitionism. "Where are Theodore D. Weld and his wife, and Sarah M. Grimké?" he asked in *The Liberator.* "All 'in the quiet' and far removed from all strife! Once the land was shaken by their free spirits, but now they are neither seen nor felt."

The sisters did not reply to this sneer; perhaps they realized that there was some truth in it. While they had not lost interest in the movement and continued to correspond and advise abolitionists around the country, they were not as active as they had been.

When Weld went off to his New York office each week, the sisters were left with their domestic burdens.

For the first time, Sarah and Angelina were learning the deeper implications of the women's rights question. Managing a family and a large household on a limited budget proved to be a full time, confining job for them. No longer sheltered by wealth and privilege, they found their days full of cooking, cleaning and child care. By the end of the day they had little time or energy left to devote to any other cause. "We were beginning to see the concrete problems involved in female equality," Angelina confided to a friend.

12

A New Age

Life on the little farm at Bellefield was not particularly happy. The Welds were plagued with financial problems, and Angelina suffered recurring illnesses. Her health did not improve with the birth of a third child, a daughter whom they named Sarah Grimke' Weld. The sudden change from a life of action to a life of menial household tasks was not easy for the sisters; restless spirits like theirs could not exist without activity and growth.

Weld was especially dissatisfied. He did not enjoy farm work as much as he had anticipated, and many times he asked himself, "What right have I to be plowing and planting while the battle over slavery rages all around me?"

His chance for activity came when abolitionist leaders called upon him to go to Washington and supervise the antislavery struggle in Congress. A dedicated little group of Senators and Representatives were fighting for the abolitionists. They needed someone in Washington to help them in their efforts, doing research for their speeches, talking to other Congressmen and informing abolitionists at home what they could do to help. Weld was the natural choice for the job.

Despite his woeful financial situation, Weld consented to go to Washington, leaving his wife and sister-in-law behind. Although it was a great burden for Angelina and Sarah to be left to manage the farm and the children by themselves, they were happy to let him go, knowing that this was just what he needed to revive his spirits.

Weld worked hard in Washington. The sisters looked forward to receiving his almost illegible letters, describing his research, the debates, the important people he had met. But a year in Washington disillusioned him. Like too many abolitionists, Weld was never a man of practical politics or compromise, and he loathed the constant bargaining and trading of votes which went on in Congress.

Returning to the farm at Bellefield, he vowed never to go back to the world of "political corruption." Abolitionism had moved into a new phase of political and legal maneuvering—a necessary step, but one which baffled the old guard abolitionists. Their talents had been better suited to the first stages of the movement: rousing speeches, grassroots organization and persuasive writing. A new breed of abolitionists had come on the scene, and the three old pioneers were wise enough to see that their contributions were no longer needed.

Yet opportunities for a new project to absorb their interests were not far off. Early in 1853 the Welds were invited to join a newly-formed socialistic community in New Jersey, Raritan Bay. Weld, Angelina and Sarah had been asked to run the community's model school. They decided to accept, feeling that this would be an exciting adventure in brotherhood and cooperation. As was the case with most utopian communities, the Raritan Bay Union was short-lived. The community acted far less harmoniously than they had hoped, and the experiment ended in little more than a year.

Weld's model school outlived the community itself. He used new approaches to education, such as group discussion among the students and discipline by persuasion rather than force (a truly novel concept for that day). Students heard some of the greatest minds of the age, such as Emerson and Thoreau, who were guest lecturers at the school. Naturally, the entire student body was thoroughly tutored in the principles of abolitionism.

Even though the school gave the Welds much happiness, life was not without its problems. For the first time in their lives, Angelina and Sarah had a disagreement which separated them. During Angelina's many illnesses, Sarah had cared for the three children and had run the household. Even though she appreciated her sister's assistance, Angelina could not help resenting Sarah's dominance over the household. Whenever Angelina would try to discipline her children, they would run to indulgent Aunt Sarah for refuge. It was only natural that the children should feel close to Sarah, since it was she who had cared for them most of their lives.

Sarah was never one to hold back an opinion or criticism, and she did not help matters with her frequent criticism of the way her sister raised the children.

"Sarah, I think that I should have complete charge of the children," Angelina finally said, as tactfully as possible. "It hurts me to see that my children are closer to their aunt than to their own mother."

Sarah was visibly hurt. "I can understand how you feel," she replied. "I realize now that I have been a burden on you and Theodore, but I will burden you no more. As soon as possible, I will move elsewhere."

Despite Angelina's urging her to stay, Sarah was determined to go. Sadly, she packed her few belongings and prepared to leave.

But leaving was not that simple. Sarah Grimke' was now sixty years old. Unwed, untrained, uneducated, where could she go? She thought of pursuing her lifelong interest in women's rights—perhaps she would write a book. But Sarah soon realized that even the women's movement had passed her by. Younger, more energetic women like Elizabeth Cady Stanton (whom Sarah had inspired) now led the feminist movement. These younger women appreciated Sarah's early contributions, but they could not now find a place for the aging pioneer. She had a few close friends, like Sarah Douglass and Lucretia Mott, but they were as old as she and had families of their own. She would only be a burden to them.

Sadly, Sarah came face to face with her situation. Writing one of her close friends she said:

At 60 I look back on a life of deep disappointments, of withered hopes, of unlooked for suffering, of severe discipline. Yet I have sometimes tasted exquisite joy and have found solace for many a woe in the innocence and earnest love of Theodore's children. But for this my life would have little to record of mundane pleasures.

There was Sarah's reason for living—"Theodore's children." The only outlets for her love, her energy and her great sensitivity were other people's children, and at sixty, without "Theodore's children" to love, care for and fret over, Sarah had nothing else to do with her life.

She had been away from the Welds for only a few weeks when Angelina wrote to her, frankly admitting that she had wronged her older sister, and begging her to return. Sarah accepted. "Separation from these darling children overwhelmed me," she said.

For the last time in Sarah Grimké's life she had been offered her independence and had been unable to accept it. She had soared as high as her times, her age and her needs would let her, and now she settled down to spend the rest of her life in contented dependency, filling the role of the old maid aunt.

Times were changing rapidly. On a warm April morning in 1860, Confederate guns on the Charleston battery were aimed across the bay at Fort Sumter. The shots fired that day signaled the beginning of the Civil War. Though they had always been pacifists, the three pioneers rallied behind the Northern banner. To them the North was not only the keeper of the Union but also the instrument to end slavery. But not all Northerners thought of themselves as emancipators. Most were more concerned with Southern rebelliousness than the freeing of the slaves. Weld criticized Lincoln for his indecision over emancipation. "The government, with Lincoln at its head, has not a heart-throb for the slave," wrote Sarah. When emancipation came, late in the war, the sisters rejoiced at this final victory for abolitionism.

During the war Weld lectured throughout New England. How strange it was for this battered old abolitionist to find his once "radical" cause now a fashionable belief. He smiled to himself to hear fat, pompous aristocrats call abolitionism the duty of all "patriotic Americans."

Angelina and Sarah contributed to the war effort by organizing women's groups to pack medical supplies and collect money for the wounded. Of greatest interest to the sisters were the newspaper accounts of the new "colored regiments" which had been enlisted, against much opposition, to fight for the Union.

Watching their friends' boys march triumphantly off to war saddened Angelina and Theodore. Their eldest son, Charles Stewart Weld, a student at Harvard, refused to serve in the war because of his pacifist convictions. Unlike his parents, he was convinced that the Civil War was immoral. Eventually Charles left for France. Like many reformer's sons, he rejected his parents' zeal for social activism.

But their greatest tragedy was the incurable illness of young Theodore, who had spent most of his life as an invalid. Sarah wondered if she had done something which had harmed Theodore as a child. The frantic parents tried everything from great doctors to medical quacks without finding a cure for his lingering illness. Eventually Theodore was sent to an institution, where he died after some years.

Their daughter, Sarah Grimke' Weld, was less trouble than the other children. She grew to be a pleasant, normal girl whose only interest in the feminist movement was her brief job as an aid in the offices of the *Women's Journal.* Eventually she married a minister, had four children, and lived out her life as a contented housewife. To Weld, Angelina and Sarah, who had struggled so long for rights, causes and reforms, the lives of their children were somewhat disappointing. Perhaps their own dominant personalities had overshadowed the children, leaving them little room for development.

Sarah and Angelina viewed the end of the bloodiest war in the nation's history with mixed emotions. The power of the South had been broken; slavery was ended.

Charleston, once their home, was in ruins. From relatives they received tragic reports of the devastated city, in the grip of disease, starvation and lawlessness. The sisters could not help feeling sadness at the fate of this once-beautiful city.

Angelina and Sarah were wise enough to know that although slavery had been abolished, the rights of the black man were not yet secure. "The former slaves will need help if they are to make it on their own," wrote Angelina at the close of the war. They began at once to collect food, money and clothing for the freed men. They were convinced that mere freedom was not enough for the black man; he must have equal education, equal rights and equal opportunities as well.

The racial problem was brought home to the Welds in a dramatic way. One evening Angelina happened to read about a meeting at Lincoln University, a college in Pennsylvania for Negro men, at which, "a student named Grimké delivered a fine address." Could he be related to them? Angelina wrote the young man a note, asking him to tell her about himself and his family. The reply came quickly.

The student wrote that he was pleased to hear from "Miss Angelina Grimké of Anti-Slavery celebrity." He explained, that, "I am the son of your brother, Henry Grimké, and therefore your nephew. My name is Archibald Grimké. My mother was Henry Grimké's slave." The practice of white masters using favored Negro slaves for mistresses was not uncommon in the South, and Archibald and his brother Frank, both students at Lincoln University, were the offspring of such a union between master and slave.

Some people might have simply tried to forget what

had happened, but not the Grimke' sisters. The two boys were invited to the Weld home in Boston and lovingly received as members of the family. For the rest of their lives, Sarah and Angelina wrote often to Archie and Frank, offering motherly advice, inquiring about their studies, sending money for their education. The boys gave their newly-discovered aunts much to be proud of. Frank graduated from Princeton Theological Seminary, eventually became pastor of a large Presbyterian church in Washington, D. C., and lived a full life as a distinguished Negro leader.

Archibald Grimke' graduated from Harvard Law School, authored many pamphlets on behalf of Negro rights, and finished his life as United States consul to Santo Domingo and vice president of the National Association for the Advancement of Colored People. He credited his aunts with having made him, "a liberal in religion, a radical in the woman suffrage movement, in politics and on the race question." He and his brother carried on the work to which their aunts had dedicated their lives, far exceeding the talents or achievements of the other Grimke' children.

As America moved into the last quarter of the nineteenth century, the feminist movement continued to gain strength. Even though Angelina and Sarah had grown old, their life-long interest in women's rights continued. The aging sisters even adopted the "Bloomer" costume, a "scandalous" outfit which consisted of a tunic and short skirt over frilled pantaloons. The costume had been advocated by Amelia Bloomer as a protest against the uncomfortable and unhealthy feminine garments of the day, with their bustles, tight stays and layers of petticoats. Bloomers became a

symbol of revolt against the confining traditional dress of women, and the term "Bloomers" stuck to the feminists as a nickname of ridicule.

But the sisters' work in the feminist cause went beyond the wearing of Bloomers. From time to time Angelina was asked to speak to women's conventions, while Sarah published an occasional article. They looked on with pride as younger women, among them Elizabeth Cady Stanton, Lucy Stone and Susan B. Anthony, attacked wage and job discrimination against women. Even their small demand to raise women's wages to just fifty or sixty percent of those of men was a radical issue in that day. The right to vote for women was still a distant dream.

13

Conclusion

Old age did not cool Sarah and Angelina Grimké's ardor for reform; they were crusaders to the very end. At seventy-nine Sarah could be seen in the streets of Boston, selling copies of John Stuart Mill's *Subjection of Women.* Both sisters were active members of the Massachusetts Woman Suffrage Association until their deaths.

On March 7, 1870, the day of the Boston city election, they joined in a public protest on behalf of women's suffrage. It was the first such protest in Massachusetts, though there would be thousands in the future. Despite the howling snowstorm that day, forty-two women, headed by Sarah, Angelina and Theodore Weld, marched to the polling place.

Blinding snow swirled around the procession. Sarah clutched her shawl and shivered against the biting wind. "How strange," she said to Angelina, "for us to be marching in the lead here today. How far away this place is from the balmy breezes of Charleston."

"The winds of fate blow in strange directions," said Weld.

"Perhaps," Angelina remarked, "yet it is right that we should be here, marching against one more area of human injustice. We have been blessed in our lives with much opportunity for service."

"And much determination to serve, my dear," said Weld, grasping Angelina's hand.

The procession trudged on toward the polling place. On one corner a little crowd had gathered to heckle the protesters. "Go back to your pots and pans!" someone shouted. The bystanders laughed in approval. It was not the first hostile crowd the Grimkés had seen.

As they approached the polls Weld distributed a small flower to each woman. Then each came forward and dropped her special "ballot" into a box. These "ballots" would not be counted because they were the votes of women, but to the aging sisters, who had been defending women's rights for over thirty years, the demonstration was a dramatic gesture of protest.

After depositing their symbolic flowers, the little band stood for a few moments in silence outside of the polling place. Night was approaching; the snow continued to fall, though the wind had subsided somewhat. As she looked out across the Boston Common, Angelina remembered that spring day many years ago, when she had entered this city for the first time, starting her career as an abolitionist agent. The same newspapers which had once ridiculed her and Sarah now hailed them as "courageous pioneers." Old customs and injustices, once seemingly unchangable, had been swept away.

"We have been fortunate," Angelina thought, "to witness the change. I wonder when there will be no injustice to fight, no more wrongs to right. I will never see that day in my lifetime – nor will any man see such a time, I suppose."

The snow muffled the sounds of the little band as

they began to disperse. The last gray light of day was fading from the Common.

"Soon it will be night," thought Angelina. "Perhaps tomorrow the sun will be shining."

THE END